YUCATÁN

Mexico's Hidden Beaches and Ruins

YUCATÁN

Mexico's Hidden Beaches and Ruins

A Traveler's Guide
by Memo Barroso

Harmony Books

Published by Harmony Books, a division of Crown Publishers, Inc., One Park Avenue, New York, New York 10016, and simultaneously in Canada by General Publishing Company Limited

HARMONY and colophon are trademarks of Crown Publishers, Inc.

Manufactured in the United States of America

Library of Congress Cataloging in Publication Data
Barroso, Memo.
Yucatán, Mexico's hidden beaches and ruins.
1. Yucatán (Mexico)—Description and travel—
Guide-books. I. Title.
F1376.B28   1983   917.2'604833   82-21200

Design by Wendy Cohen

ISBN: 0-517-54789-9

10 9 8 7 6 5 4 3

First Edition

To André Sala

Contents

ACKNOWLEDGMENTS   ix
INTRODUCTION   1

YUCATÁN STATE

MÉRIDA   24
UXMAL   43
CHICHÉN ITZÁ   45
SAN FELIPE   48
RÍO LAGARTOS   50

QUINTANA ROO STATE

ISLA HOLBOX   58
ISLA MUJERES   64
CANCÚN   79
PUERTO MORELOS   108
PUNTA BETE   112
PLAYA DEL CARMEN   119
COZUMEL   123
HIDDEN BEACHES OPPOSITE COZUMEL   146
TULUM   158
COBÁ   164

APPENDIX

FOOD GUIDE   168
FIRST AID   179
USEFUL SPANISH EXPRESSIONS   182

Acknowledgments

I wish to express my deepest gratitude to the following people whose help was invaluable in producing this book: Pamela Prince; Anita Sala; my mother, Consuelo; my brothers Jorge and Roberto; Raul De La Sota; Francisco, Josefina, Lupita, Juanito, and Pablito Clavijo; Toño and Josefina Garcia; Toño and Elena Nieto; Eduardo Villar; Janet Sonntag; Sandy Foreman; and Patricia Drake.

Special thanks to Dr. Glen Ammerman from Austin, Texas, for his help with the information on health care, and to divers Francisco Contreras (Cozumel), Gerardo Buzo (Cancún), and Fernando Cusi (Puerto Morelos).

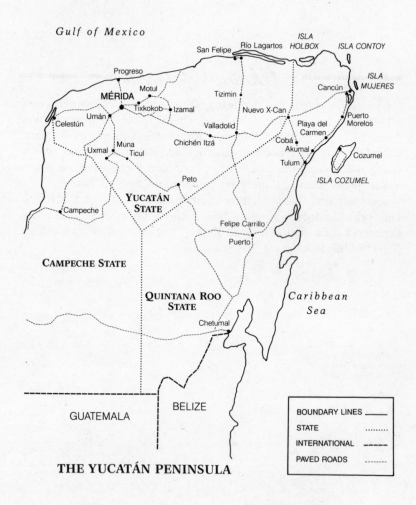

THE YUCATÁN PENINSULA

Introduction

The Yucatán Peninsula

The Yucatán Peninsula is located in southeastern Mexico and has a surface area of 61,546 square miles. Politically, the peninsula is divided into three states: Campeche in the western part, Yucatán to the north, and Quintana Roo to the east. This book deals with the states of Yucatán and Quintana Roo.

The Yucatán Peninsula is for the most part as flat as the Caribbean Sea that surrounds it. Apart from the hilly areas of the central region, with altitudes of under 700 feet, the highest points are either pyramid tops, church bell towers, or hotel penthouses.

Bordered on the west and north coasts by the Gulf of Mexico and on the east (Quintana Roo) by the Caribbean Sea, the Yucatán Peninsula has over a thousand miles of coastline. The beaches on the Caribbean Sea, because of their sugar-white sand, transparent turquoise waters, and sleepy coconut trees, are by far the most appealing of the peninsula.

The People and the Language

The Mexican people of today are the result of over 450 years of blending of Spanish and Indian ethnic groups. *Mestizo* is the name given to the people of this ethnic blend. But the family origins of most Mexicans are lost in the chromosomes of history, and to indicate their origin, Mexicans will proudly mention their region and the state where they were born rather than their backgrounds.

Some groups of the Mexican population, however, have remained predominantly Indian—the Mayans in the Yucatán Peninsula, for example. Present-day Mayans still live much as their ancestors did, and their strongest link to their past is the Mayan language, which is perhaps as widely spoken in this area as Spanish, Mexico's official language.

1

Nevertheless, as they become involved in Mexico's social, educational, economic, and industrial development, they are inevitably speaking more Spanish.

Glossary

Avenida avenue
Calesa horse-drawn carriage
Calle street
Cenote the large natural wells found in the peninsula
Concha seashell
Guayabera typical Yucatecán man's shirt
Henequen sisal
Huipil the typical, colorful dress worn by Mayan women
Isla island
Larga Distancia long distance (telephone)
Malecón an avenue running next to the sea (Isla Mujeres and Cozumel)
Palapa thatched roof made from coconut tree leaves or other palm-tree leaves
Retorno U-shaped streets common in Cancún
Iva the 15 percent tax charged in the better hotels and restaurants
Leeward the side of an island protected from waves and winds
Windward the side of an island exposed to strong waves and winds

Climate

In the Yucatán Peninsula, as in other tropical regions of Mexico, there are two seasons—the hot one and the very hot one.

From November to March, temperatures are in the 80- to 95-degree range in the coastal areas and slightly higher in the interior. For instance, when it is 85 degrees in Cancún, it is usually 90 in Chichén Itzá. During this season there are a few days of cloudy and rainy weather, which are a side effect of cold weather fronts in the United States and Canada. As a result, temperatures occasionally cool down to 70 to 75 degrees.

The month of May is a particularly hot one and announces with blasting heat the beginning of the very humid rainy season. From May through September there are regular afternoon showers and the temperatures climb into the 90s. The weather is hot, steamy, and ideal for turning people into walking tamales.

But some like it hot and remember that as the temperatures go up, hotel prices go down. Places like Cancún, Cozumel, and Isla Mujeres are almost empty of tourists during this time of the year and you will seldom get better service in hotels and restaurants.

Water and Cenotes

The combined yearly average rainfall for the states of Yucatán and Quintana Roo is 46 inches. But the peninsula's flat terrain and the thirsty limestone that forms it do not favor the formation of lakes and streams. There are a few rivers in the southern part of the peninsula—the main one being Río Hondo, which separates Quintana Roo from Belize.

The main source for the supply of fresh water for the peninsula's towns and cities is found in the natural wells and underground rivers called *cenotes* in Mayan. *Cenotes* are as important here as oases are in the desert and were vital in the development of Mayan civilization. In fact, some archaeologists theorize that the downfall of Mayan civilization was due to a prolonged drought that affected the growing of crops and possibly caused the drying up of water supplies in *cenotes.*

Vegetation

The peninsula's rocky and shallow soil formation can only support a vegetation of low brush, cacti, and lonely trees that will gladly trade their shade for a little company. People work as hard as bees in this largely unproductive land—almost literally so, since the peninsula is one of the world's leading producers of honey.

The henequen plantations, covering hundreds of square miles around the Mérida area, are an important feature of the vegetation found in the peninsula. Henequen, or sisal, is a cactus of the agave family, and its long, fibrous leaves, measuring about 2 feet in length, are processed to make rope. The dry, hot climate and the

Mexican Holidays and "Puentes"

Millions of Mexicans live and work in urban areas such as Mexico City, with its twelve or thirteen or who knows how many million inhabitants.

The tensions and pressures of city life are like a great storm that builds up and finally unchains itself during the holiday periods. Then huge waves of vacationers from the storm's centers—Mexico City, Guadalajara, Puebla—hit beach resorts all over Mexico, flooding buses, trains, airplanes, hotels, and restaurants. These human storms are very predictable and occur during Semana Santa (Easter Week) and Navidad (Christmas).

Foreign vacationers planning to visit Mexico during these holiday periods are advised to make transportation and hotel reservations three to four months before their visit.

Puentes, literally meaning "bridges," have become a tradition among bureaucrats and white- and blue-collar workers. Let's assume, for example, that a Thursday happens to be a legal holiday. This day automatically becomes a pillar of the bridge, with Saturday and Sunday being the other pillar. The temptation to leave the bridge unfinished is too great, and thousands of workers will add the missing span by getting Friday off, thus becoming architects of their vacation bridges.

The legal Mexican holidays are the following:
January 1, New Year's Day
February 5, Flag Day
March 21, Nationalization of the Oil Industry
May 1, Labor Day
May 5, Battle of Puebla
September 16, Independence Day
October 12, Columbus Day
November 20, Anniversary of the Revolution
December 12, Our Lady of Guadalupe (not a legal holiday, but nevertheless celebrated throughout the country)
December 25, Christmas Day
Puentes, however, will rarely affect your traveling plans.

rocky terrain are ideal for growing this cactus and its cultivation and processing are Yucatán State's main source of income.

In areas with deep, rich topsoil, the vegetation doesn't simply grow; it climbs, twists, and digs, and plants grow on top of other plants. These are the tropical forests that cover vast areas of Yucatán and Quintana Roo states. Mahogany, rosewood, and other precious woods come from the tropical forests of Quintana Roo State, where timber is one of the major industries.

Wildlife

The Yucatán Peninsula has an immensely rich wildlife. Deer, armadillos, tapir, wild boar, land turtles, anteaters, iguanas, and monkeys are among the most common land animals. Besides its dozens of indigenous species of land and water birds, the peninsula is a crossroads for countless migratory birds.

The numerous reefs in the eastern part of the peninsula provide an ideal habitat for over 100 species of tropical fish, not to mention the many species of deep-sea fish and other inhabitants such as turtles, rays, and eels.

Check the bird-watching, beachcombing, fishing, snorkeling, and scuba-diving sections of this guide for more detailed information on particular birds, fish, shell, and coral species found in the waters that surround the Yucatán Peninsula.

Getting There

AIRPLANE

Flights to the Yucatán Peninsula arrive at the international airports at Cancún, Cozumel, and Mérida. Direct flights from the United States to Mérida and Cancún depart from Houston, Los Angeles, Miami, New York, Chicago, and New Orleans, and direct flights to Cozumel from Chicago, New York, Houston, and Miami.

Aeromexico, Mexicana, Continental, Eastern, and United Airlines fly to the Yucatán Peninsula. Before buying your ticket from an airline, check with your travel agent for the best deal on excursions, off-season promotions, and vacation packages.

Remember to make your airline reservations about 6 months ahead of time for the high season (December through March).

─────────────────── **BUS** ───────────────────

Mexico has an extensive bus system connecting every city in the country with even the smallest and remotest village.

Mexican buses are inexpensive and some first-class lines have buses as comfortable as those in the United States and Canada. Keep in mind, however, that the Yucatán Peninsula is the farthest region of Mexico to reach by land from United States border points. For example, the distance from Brownsville at the Texas-Mexico border to Mérida in Yucatán State, is 1,400 miles, and from Tijuana at the California-Mexico border to Mérida is 2,723 miles. These distances translate to approximately 48 and 72 hours of bus-riding time. Obviously then, a bus trip through Mexico to the Yucatán Peninsula should be undertaken only by those with time to spare and money to save.

Here are a few pointers for bus travelers in Mexico, particularly in the Yucatán Peninsula:

1. Mexican bus tickets are not open-dated—they are valid for a specific hour and day. If you miss the bus, you lose your money.

2. In first-class and on most second-class bus lines, you will get a numbered bus seat. You may pick the seat of your choice: *ventanilla* (window) or *pasillo* (aisle).

3. First-class buses are slightly more expensive than second-class and are generally faster and more comfortable.

4. There is a lot of passenger traffic between Cancún-Valladolid-Mérida and Cancún-Tulum-Chetumal on weekends and at long holiday periods such as Christmas and Easter. Buy your bus ticket at least one to two days ahead of time during these periods.

5. Do not drink too many liquids before a long trip unless you are sure that your bus has a toilet or that it makes frequent stops.

There are about a dozen bus lines servicing the Yucatán Peninsula, and there is hardly a town or archaeological site that cannot be reached by bus. ADO first-class service connects Mérida, Cancún, and other cities in the peninsula with Mexico City and points in between. Autotransportes del Caribe and Unión de Camioneros de Yucatán have first- and second-class buses and service all major cities and towns in the peninsula.

All cities have a central bus station (Central de Autobúses) where all bus lines converge.

─────────────────── **CAR** ───────────────────

The most pleasant way to see Mexico and the Yucatán Peninsula is by car. A car gives you the freedom to reach remote villages, ruins, and hidden beaches; to stop when and where you want; and best of all to carry the camping, diving, and fishing equipment that will make your vacation more enjoyable. However, driving in Mexico requires extra caution, attention, and patience. You will have to contend with narrow, two-lane roads without shoulders, stretches of road filled with potholes, inadequate road signs, animals grazing on the road's edge, and of course, careless drivers.

Road traffic is heavy on the main roads between the United States border and the city of Campeche, on the western side of the Yucatán Peninsula, but traffic thins down considerably once you start to drive into the peninsula proper. For safer driving, keep in mind the following hints.

1. Avoid driving at night.

2. Keep your speed under 50 mph (75 km per hour) on two-way roads. The speed limit in cities is 40 mph (60 kph) unless otherwise marked.

3. Keep a constant eye on your rearview mirror, especially before passing a slow vehicle.

4. Always slow down when approaching a narrow bridge *(puente angosto)*. The rule, supposedly, is that the vehicle closest to the bridge has the right of way. Don't trust this rule.

5. *Topes* are concrete or asphalt bumps designed to slow down traffic through towns. Keep an eye out for *topes* as they are not always marked.

Car Insurance American and Canadian insurance policies are not valid in Mexico, but you can buy short-term insurance at border towns as you cross into Mexico. If you are a member of the American Automobile Association (AAA), you can buy Mexican car insurance at the same rates you would get at the border. The AAA is also a valuable source of good Mexican road maps and travel information.

Fuel Pemex *(Petróleos Mexicanos)* is the only oil company found throughout Mexico and is controlled by the Mexican government. Gas stations are found everywhere and generally there is no problem getting gas. Occasionally though, in Quintana Roo State on the eastern part of the peninsula, gas stations may run out of gas during heavy vacation periods. Always fill up with gas when you have a quarter of a tank left. There are two types of gas available in Mexico—Nova (81 octane leaded gasoline) selling for 20 pesos a liter and Extra (94 octane unleaded gasoline) at 30 pesos a liter. There are 3.8 liters in a gallon. In many regions of Mexico, including the Yucatán Peninsula, it is difficult to get Extra (unleaded) gasoline. It is therefore highly advisable to drive to Mexico in a car that uses leaded gasoline.

Your Car's Mechanical Condition The best way to avoid mechanical problems is to have your car in top shape before leaving on your long trip to the Yucatán Peninsula. If you are capable of making minor car repairs, pack your own tools and some spare parts such as a fan belt, a condenser, points, spark plugs, etc. Some car brands are not sold in Mexico (Volvo, Mazda, Honda, Fiat, Cadillac, Pontiac, and Oldsmobile are among them) and you could run into serious complications getting replacement parts in the event of a breakdown.

Car Rentals Cars can be rented in Cancún, Mérida, and Cozumel from American and Mexican companies. Although their rates are roughly the same, it is still wise to shop around for weekly rates, special mileage deals, and the newest cars available in order to avoid mechanical problems.

When renting a car, do not assume that it is in good shape simply because you are renting it from a well-known company. Make sure all tires are in good shape and remember that the spare is only spare until you need it. Make sure it has air. Check the jack, windshield wipers, door locks, and hand brake, and simply pretend that you are buying rather than renting the car.

Your American or Canadian driver's license is valid when driving Mexican rental cars.

TRAIN

Trains are minitowns on wheels and can be an interesting way to see the country and rub shoulders with its people. But trains in Mexico are as slow as inchworms and should be taken for the experience of the ride rather than for speedy transportation.

There is a train service from United States points to Mexico City and from there to Mérida.

Entry Requirements and Customs

American and Canadian visitors to Mexico need a tourist card. To obtain one you must have proof of citizenship. Birth certificate, valid passport, voter's registration card, naturalization papers, or armed-services discharge papers are acceptable. A driver's license is not valid for this purpose.

Tourist cards can be obtained at the following places:

1. Mexican consulates in major American and Canadian cities.
2. Offices of the Mexican National Tourist Council in major American and Canadian cities.
3. Authorized airline offices.
4. Mexican immigration offices at point of entry.

Tourist cards are issued free of charge and are valid for up to 6 months. When you obtain your tourist card, it is advisable to ask for more time than you need as a precaution against delayed or lost flights, illness, car problems, etc.

It is usually difficult to obtain extension permits unless you can prove that you are in an emergency situation. Often the easiest way to obtain additional time in Mexico is to leave the country and obtain a new tourist card as you return. From the Yucatán Peninsula this can be done by visiting Belize.

When traveling with their parents, children under 15 can be included on one parent's tourist card. But take note: a parent cannot leave the country alone if children are included on his or her tourist card. To avoid any complications in case of separate departures, request individual tourist cards for each member of the family.

To travel alone in Mexico, minors under 18 need a notarized affidavit in duplicate, certifying that the parents or legal guardians authorize their trip. Birth certificate or naturalization papers will also be necessary to obtain the tourist card.

All visitors must turn in their tourist cards to the authorities when leaving Mexico. In case of loss or theft of your tourist card, contact the nearest immigration office. There are Mexican immigration offices in Mérida, Cancún, Isla Mujeres, and Cozumel.

Visitors may take into Mexico the following items duty free: up to 110 pounds of clothing and personal articles; one camera, one movie camera, and 12 rolls of film for each; used sporting equip-

Tax

Impuesto is the Spanish word for tax, and it's interesting to note that it comes from the Spanish verb *imponer,* "to impose."

In Mexico, there is a 15 percent tax on any item or expense considered nonessential, for example, liquor, film, the better hotels and restaurants, fishing trips, guided tours, and so on. This tax is called IVA (translated as added value tax) and it's more a luxury than a sales tax.

To avoid paying this tax, shop in marketplaces, craft markets, small grocery stores, and buy from street vendors; eat in small, inexpensive restaurants, and stay in the cheaper hotels.

ment; 200 cigarettes, 50 cigars, or 9 ounces of loose tobacco (adults only); and professional equipment or instruments for personal use.

To take vehicles, trailers, and boats into Mexico you must obtain a Temporary Importation Permit at your border entry point. To obtain this permit you will need proof of ownership, state registration card, valid license plates, and valid driver's license.

Temporary Importation Permits are issued free of charge and are valid for the same period of time as the vehicle owner's tourist card. The temporary importation of a vehicle into Mexico is noted on your tourist card, and you cannot leave the country without it. In the event that you should need to leave Mexico without your vehicle, you must leave it in the custody of customs and you will be charged a storage fee.

Boat owners must pay a small monthly fee for boats under 22 feet in length and must place a customs bond for boats over 22 feet.

What to Bring

The weather in the Yucatán Peninsula is ideal for wearing nothing but a big smile, but it is nevertheless advisable to wear some clothes to match it. Here are a few tips to help you choose your wardrobe.

1. Wear lightweight, light-colored fabrics—dark colors soak up the sun.

2. Wear cotton and cotton-blend fabrics. Clothes made entirely out of synthetic fibers do not "breathe" and are hot and sticky.

3. Wear loose pants. Tight designer jeans will make you look sexy, but as you sweat you will feel like a wet banana in its skin.

4. Take a sweater for cool nights in the winter months.

5. Take lightweight rain gear for the rainy season (May through September) and the winter months (December through March).

6. Take a hat and sandals for the beach and sturdy walking shoes for the ruins.

If you wish to travel light and shop for clothes in Mexico, clothing stores and craft markets in Cancún, Cozumel, and Mérida offer a wide selection of beachwear, original design clothes, and typical Mexican clothes such as *huipiles,* the colorful, loose dresses worn by Mayan women, and *guayaberas,* the typical Yucatecán shirt.

The sun is extremely hot in the Yucatán. Bring sunscreen, suntan lotion, sunglasses, and a hat. Check the First-Aid section (page 179) in case you get too much sun.

Feel free to bring your own fishing, snorkeling, etc. equipment. If you would rather travel light, don't worry—there are plenty of places to rent equipment.

The Naked Truth

The closer you get to the equator, the hotter you'll be and the more you'll want to shed your clothes. In most public beaches in the Yucatán Peninsula, anytime you totally expose yourself below your own equator, you run the risk of creating a hot situation. The only public beach on the peninsula where total nudity seems to be tolerated is El Mirador, about a mile south of the ruins at Tulum. Even there, though, it's always recommended to keep your clothes close at hand. In public beaches in Cozumel, Cancún, and Isla Mujeres, topless sunbathing is not legal but it's tolerated as long as it's discreet.

For women wishing to sunbathe topless at public beaches, the problem usually is not offending morals, but rather attracting curious and obnoxious male onlookers.

Avoid nude sunbathing around Mexican families, drunks, and in crowds made up mostly of Mexicans.

Ceiling Fans

Throughout the Yucatán Peninsula, budget-priced hotels are usually equipped with ceiling fans instead of air conditioning. The advantages of ceiling fans are obvious. They cool you, provide air circulation, and make you feel as if you were sleeping outdoors, simply by your adjusting the fan to your favorite setting: gentle breeze, rude breeze, gale, whale of a gale, or hurricane.

But if you are 6 feet tall or more, ceiling fans can sometimes be a cause for concern. Here is a list of precautions to take when you check into a hotel room equipped with a ceiling fan and you feel like a helpless carrot inside a gigantic Cuisinart.

1. The tallest person in your party should check to make sure that the fan cannot be touched with arms outstretched. (Make sure the fan is off first.)

2. If the fan is low enough to make you worry, put under it suitcases, backpacks, table, chairs, beach bums, or anything that will keep you from stepping into the area below it.

3. Be careful when handling long objects such as fishing rods, spear guns, and when shaking clothes.

4. If the fan is over your bed, make a note of it, and when you wake up in the morning, *do not stand on the bed* to stretch. Under the circumstances, it is better to go unstretched all day.

If your height excludes you from this problem, you need only remember not to invite basketball players to your room.

Where to Stay

In these sections most or all of the hotels, motels, cabañas, bunga-lows, *palapas,* or rental houses are listed. For quick reference they are grouped into three price ranges (for a double room):

Budget: to 1,000 pesos
Moderate: 1,000 to 2,000 pesos
Deluxe: above 2,000 pesos
Even when the present rates become outdated due to price

increases, this classification system can still be used to compare value for money.

The rates quoted are for double occupancy without meals during the high season. Single rates are generally about one-quarter cheaper and triple rates about one-quarter higher than the double rate. Remember, every effort has been made to obtain accurate rates, but it is up to you to check out the cost.

Reservations It is recommended that you make reservations well ahead of time for busy holiday periods—Christmas season, from around December 20 to January 5, and Easter week. Reservations can be made by phone, by writing to the address given for each hotel, or by contacting your travel agent. Most hotels in the budget range do not take reservations.

European vs. American Plan Briefly, the European Plan is a room without meals and the American Plan is a room with meals. The European Plan gives you the freedom to eat what you want, when you want, and where you want. The American Plan can save you money, but limits you to eating what you are served (the choice of dishes is usually limited), when you are served (there are specific serving hours), and always in the same restaurant. Also, under this plan there is usually no refund or credit for meals not taken.

Go Bananas

Bananas are usually called *plátanos* in Mexico. But in certain regions of Mexico and other Latin American countries they are also *bananas.*

The type of banana sold in the United States and Canadian market is known in Mexico as *tabasco.* A slightly shorter and chubbier variety is known as *manzano,* while a tiny banana about 3 inches long is known as *dominico.* The largest banana of them all is about a foot long and is known as *macho* in Mexico, while in North America it's called plantain. This banana is usually eaten fried or baked.

Although most bananas are yellow, the exception is a chubby purple banana known as *morado.* This is the tastiest of them all. Try it and go bananas.

Restaurants

Restaurants in this book are also listed in order of the cheapest to the most expensive. For each restaurant listed, I have indicated the name, address, telephone number (for the better ones), types of food served, personal observations, and the approximate cost. In most cases I have estimated the cost of a medium-priced meal consisting of soup or salad and main course plus a beer or a glass of wine. Lunches cost about the same as dinners unless you take advantage of inexpensive *comida corridas* (lunch specials) offered in budget restaurants in downtown Mérida, Cancún, and Cozumel.

Papadzules, poc-chuc, and chicken *pibil* are Yucatecán food specialties, but it's all Mayan to you unless you know what ingredients they contain and how they are prepared.

The Food Guide on page 168 gives you a detailed description of the most common Yucatecán and Mexican specialties.

Beaches and Activities

BEACH HIKING/CAMPING

The beaches chosen for hiking/camping are uninhabited, easily accessible, very private, and offer a number of activities such as snorkeling, fishing, beachcombing, and bird-watching.

The hiking distances are between 2 and 10 miles round trip, depending on the beach, and the terrain is flat, sandy beach and/or rocky shoreline.

In all cases, hikers and campers must take food and water necessary for the duration of their stay.

BEACHCOMBING

Beachcombing is a relaxing pastime that can be practiced by anyone taking a walk on the beach. In the Yucatán Peninsula, the best shell beachcombing beaches are located in Yucatán State on the northern part of the peninsula in places like Isla Holbox, Río Lagartos, San Felipe, and Progreso. Clams, cockles, cowries, conches, and cones are among the several groups of shells found here. The beaches between Xelhá and Akumal in Quintana Roo State are excellent beachcomber areas for various species of coral.

Wear good sunglasses as protection from the sun's reflection on the bright, white sand.

Tanning Tips

Every day hundreds of pale sun worshipers arrive in the Yucatán Peninsula to make offerings of peeled skin to the great sun god. Use the following guidelines to keep yourself from looking like a shedding snake:

1. The longer it has been since you last were in the sun, the more likely you are to burn.

2. The lighter and drier your skin is, the faster you can burn.

3. The sun's burning rays are more intense between 10:00 A.M. and 3:00 P.M.

4. Sunscreens allow you to stay out in the sun for a longer period of time than your skin type would tolerate. For instance, a sunscreen with a "1" protection factor means that you can stay in the sun twice as long as your skin would normally tolerate.

5. Suntan products help to promote a tan, but may not contain a protective sunscreen.

6. Be careful not to fall asleep in the sun.

7. If possible, start your tan before arriving.

8. The sun's burning rays penetrate through the ocean's surface. Wear a T-shirt when you are swimming and snorkeling.

BIRD-WATCHING

The Yucatán Peninsula is an area of Mexico with an extremely rich and varied bird life, and a trip here for the sole purpose of watching and photographing birds would be well worth your time and money. It is easy to combine bird-watching with other vacation activities. Birds are everywhere as you go pyramid climbing at Cobá or Uxmal, sight-seeing around Cozumel Island, fishing at Boca Paila, or beachcombing at San Felipe. And if you're lying on the beach, just look up and you might discover a magnificent frigate bird flying overhead.

The basic purpose of the bird-watching sections of this guide is to give amateur bird-watchers some idea of where to go and what species they might find there.

If you are serious about bird-watching and wish to identify the species you see, you should equip yourself with one of the field guides to Mexican birds available in bookstores in the United States and Canada. I used *A Field Guide to Mexican Birds* by Roger Tory Peterson and Edward Chalif and the *Audubon Water Bird Guide* by Richard H. Pough to identify the birds mentioned in this book.

I often regretted not having with me a field guide for birds from countries north of Mexico to identify the countless migratory bird species that spend winters in the Yucatán singing, fishing, sight-seeing, and hopping from branch to branch and beach to beach.

Ouch and Itch

Every human being is a blood bank and every square inch of exposed skin is a teller's window from which mosquitoes can draw funds to their hearts' content.

Save your blood for the Red Cross and take the following precautions against mosquitoes:

1. Don't be a sucker by thinking that mosquitoes won't get you. Wear long pants, sleeves, socks, and a scarf around your neck after sunset, particularly near swampy areas.

2. Put on a good mosquito repellent.

3. When camping, stay as close as possible to the beach. Generally, the breeze will keep mosquitoes safely away.

CAMPING

There are about a dozen paying campgrounds in the area between Cancún and Tulum, 80 miles south. Most are clean and offer basic facilities (rest rooms, showers, and an adequate supply of water). There are also numerous desolate beach stretches that are accessible by car and are ideal for camping.

Backpackers will find useful information to plan their camping trips in the Beach Hiking/Camping sections of this guide.

American-style trailer parks are scarce in the Yucatán Peninsula. There are trailer parks in Mérida, Pisté (next to Chichén Itzá) and Punta Sam (next to Cancún). However, some campgrounds in the beach area between Cancún and Tulum are large enough to accommodate several mobile homes. Trailer parks often have an area for use by backpackers.

Fishing Calendar

Amberjack	July to November
Barracuda	All year
Billfish	March to September
Cobia	October to December
Dorado	March to May
Groupers	All year
Shark	All year
Sierra	October to December
Tunas	July to November
Wahoo	All year (scarce)

The months from March to July are the best time for big-game fishing, while August to February are good for mostly smaller fish species.

FISHING

There are about a thousand miles of coastline in the Yucatán Peninsula, and in its warm waters there are billions of fish of many species waiting for your bait and lures. Jacks, snappers, groupers, grunts, and pompanos can be found just off the shore.

Fishing equipment is expensive and hard to find in Mexico. For shore fishing, come prepared with an adequate assortment of hooks, sinkers, wire leaders, 10-to-20-pound-test fishing lines, rods, and reels. A few spoons, plugs, and feather jigs will also come in handy for casting or trolling.

Large fishing-tackle stores in the United States and Canada are usually well acquainted with the fishing equipment you will need in the Yucatán Peninsula. I recommend that you pay them a visit before leaving home.

In fishing towns such as Río Lagartos, San Felipe, and Playa del Carmen, fishing arrangements can be made with local fishermen. You will need some knowledge of Spanish to communicate.

Deep-sea fishing boats are available in Cancún, Cozumel, Isla Mujeres, and a few smaller towns. Arrangements for deep-sea fishing can be made for a half day or a full day, and the boat operators will furnish all the tackle and bait that you will need for sailfish, marlins, dorado, and other deep-sea species. For additional information on rates, boat sizes, and fishing calendar, please read the individual deep-sea fishing sections.

For lagoon fishing, the Boca Paila lagoons, 20 miles south of the Tulum ruins, are a prime fishing spot for permit, tarpon, snook, and bonefish. But this type of fishing requires that you come well equipped with tackle and a boat.

A fishing lodge, the Pez Maya, operates at Boca Paila and accepts guests only through its fishing-lodging-transportation package.

Common Spanish Fish Names

The following is a list of the most common Spanish fish names. Commercial species such as red snapper (huachinango) usually have one name throughout the entire country. Lesser-known species such as triggerfish often have as many different names as there are regions in the country.

Albacore *Albacore*	Parrotfish *Perico, pez loro*
Ballyhoo, Balao *Escribano*	Pompano *Palometa*
Barracuda *Barracuda*	Porgy *Mojarra*
Bass *Cabrilla*	Red snapper *Huachinango*
Bonefish *Macabí*	Roosterfish *Pez gallo*
Catfish *Bagre*	Sailfish *Pez vela*
Dorado *Dorado*	Sardine *Sardina*
Grouper *Cherna*	Sea bass *Mero*
Jack *Jurel*	Snapper *Pargo*
Mackerel *Sierra*	Snook *Robálo*
Marlin *Marlín*	Swordfish *Pez espada*
Mojarra *Mojarra*	Tarpon *Sábalo*
Mullet *Lisa*	Triggerfish *Pez puerco, bota*
Needlefish *Picuda*	Tuna *Atún*

—————— SCUBA DIVING ——————

Cozumel has long been known as one of the world's scuba-diving paradises, but Palancar, Santa Rosa, and Paraiso are only a few of the reefs found along the eastern coast of the Yucatán Peninsula. From Contoy Island, on the northeastern corner of the peninsula, to the Belize border on its southeastern corner, is a reef chain some

300 miles in length. Add to this an abundant sea life, up to 250 feet visibility, and 75- to 80-degree water temperatures and you come up with perfect diving conditions.

Dive shops throughout the United States and Canada organize diving excursions to Cozumel, Isla Mujeres, Akumal, Puerto Morelos, and Tulum. If you like to travel with groups, these excursions can be a good deal, as the rate includes round-trip air fare, hotel, some meals, tanks, and a number of dive trips. Bring your certification card, as no dive shop here will rent or fill tanks without it.

If you're going to try scuba-diving for the first time, you can take a resort course at either Cancún, Cozumel, Isla Mujeres, or Akumal. The resort course is approximately 4 hours long and is an introductory course to skin diving. On completion of the course your instructor will take you on a 1-tank dive to a depth of about 20 feet. The resort course costs about $20 and is not a certification course.

SNORKELING

Going to the Yucatán Peninsula without a diving mask, snorkel, and fins is like going to a tennis court without tennis balls, shoes, and racquet. A snorkeling set will give you many hours of pleasurable underwater sight-seeing and will not add much weight to your luggage. In Mexico snorkeling gear costs about twice as much as in the United States.

Cozumel, Isla Mujeres, Xelhá, and dozens of other spots in the state of Quintana Roo in the Yucatán Peninsula have some of the world's clearest waters. Don't miss the opportunity of discovering the underwater world of French angelfish, rainbow parrotfish, queen triggerfish, blueheads, and dozens of other tropical fish.

Guide to Corals and Fishes by Idaz and Jerry Greenberg is a waterproof book that can help you identify the 200 or so species of fish that inhabit Mexico's Caribbean waters. It can be bought at some of the dive shops in Cancún and Cozumel and at the Don Quijote bookstore on Avenida Tulum in Cancún.

A to Z

Each chapter in this book has an A to Z section with specific information on airports, airlines, bank locations and their business hours, tourist information, important telephone numbers and addresses, postal and communications offices.

Don't Leave Home Without It

When traveling in Mexico, remember to include among your important papers—passport, traveler's checks, etc.—a roll or two of toilet paper. Make a habit of this and you will never regret it, as toilet paper is anywhere from absent to nonexistent in most bus stations and cheaper restaurants.

BANKS

Banking hours throughout Mexico are from 9:00 A.M. to 1:30 P.M., Monday through Friday. Most banks will readily exchange American currency and traveler's checks, but some will not exchange Canadian currency. To get the best rate of exchange, exchange your money or traveler's checks in banks. Exchange houses, hotels, and restaurants usually give less than the official exchange rate.

Traveler's checks are readily accepted in tourist areas throughout Mexico. Before buying them, check to see which companies offer the best service in the Yucatán Peninsula. The more refund offices a company has here, the better for you, in case of loss or theft.

All major credit cards are accepted in the better restaurants, hotels, and shops in the Yucatán Peninsula. With some credit cards it is possible to make cash withdrawals from major Mexican banks.

The peso is the Mexican currency unit, and it is divided into 100 centavos. Coins are minted in 20 and 50 centavos, and 1-, 5-, 10-, and 20-peso denominations. Peso bills are printed in the following denominations and colors: 20 (red); 50 (blue); 100 (purple); 500 (green); 1,000 (brown); and 5,000 pesos (red and green).

Modern Mexico lives under internal and external pressures to industrialize and develop to the full capacity its human and natural resources. As a result of this process, 50 to 75 percent annual inflation has become a part of Mexico's economic reality. Nevertheless, despite inflation, travel in Mexico is still much cheaper than in Europe, the United States, or Canada. The peso continues to "float" to a level which, if anything, increases the purchasing power of United States and Canadian dollars in Mexico. Because the peso fluctuates so much against the dollar, the costs of hotels, restaurants, etc. are given in pesos. Check the foreign exchange column of your local newspaper to obtain the current rate of exchange. I have tried to be as accurate as possible when giving prices, but it is up to you to check the cost of hotels, car rentals, etc.

The average foreign traveler in Mexico can easily afford a standard of accommodation and dining superior to what he could buy with the same amount of money in his own country.

—— POST OFFICE, TELEGRAPH, AND TELEPHONE —— SERVICES

Post and telegraph offices are located next to each other in Mérida, Cancún, Isla Mujeres, and Cozumel. Small towns, for the most part, do not have either of these services.

Air-mail rates for the United States and Canada are 13 pesos for letters and postcards. Telegrams with a maximum of 10 words cost 15 pesos within Mexico and 1,000 pesos to the United States and Canada for a maximum of 15 words. In Mexico you may receive mail and telegrams through general delivery in the local post office. Your mail should be addressed to Your Name; Lista de Correos; City, State, Mexico. Telegrams and money orders should be addressed to Your Name; Lista de Telégrafos; City, State, Mexico. Letters, telegrams, and money orders are held for 10 days before they are returned to sender.

Local and long-distance services are fairly efficient in the main cities. Long-distance calls can be made easily when you are a guest in the better hotels. Budget hotels do not offer long-distance service.

National and international long-distance calls can be made from special long-distance offices *(larga distancia)* operated by the Mexican Telephone Company. Cities and towns have one or more *larga distancia* offices depending on their size.

There will be long lines of people waiting to make calls at long-distance offices. While you wait for your turn, read the Useful Spanish Expressions section of this book, so you can communicate with the clerks who will process your call. Often they do not speak English.

YUCATÁN STATE

Río Lagartos

San Felipe

Gulf of Mexico

Progreso
Dzilam Bravo

Chelem
Chicxulub Puerto

Sisal
Motul
Tizimin

Hunucma
MÉRIDA

Tixkokob
Izamal

Umán
Hoctún
Kantunil

Celestún
Pisté
Valladolid

Chichén Itzá

Muna
YUCATÁN STATE

Uxmal

Peto

Mérida

Mérida (population: 500,000), the capital of Yucatán State, was founded in 1542 by Francisco Montejo on the site of the ancient Mayan city of Tihoo. Also known as the white city, Mérida is one of Mexico's oldest and most pleasant colonial cities and since its foundation has been the most important economic, industrial, and cultural center of the Yucatán Peninsula.

By day Mérida has the personality of a hyperactive boom town. Trucks and buses rush and rumble through the narrow downtown streets, loading and unloading cargo and passengers and creating traffic jams. People crowd the banks, shops, and restaurants, and the activity in the market place is so feverish that one gets the impression that the whole city is shopping, fearful that the market will be closed for a week. But it isn't so, *mañana* will be just as busy.

By night Mérida takes on an easygoing casual personality that fits in well with the colonial character of its streets. People relax in outdoor cafés. As they sit and people-watch they fight the lingering heat with tall glasses of fruit drinks, bottles of cold Montejo beer, and bowls of fresh fruit salad. Others stroll in the streets or in the main plaza or line up for the movies. Mérida takes its work as seriously as it takes its social life. So the city goes to sleep early, and by 10:00 P.M. the streets are almost deserted.

Mérida has a numbered street system that makes it easy to find your way around. Even-numbered streets *(calles)* run north to south, odd-numbered streets run east to west. All streets downtown are one way. The heart of town, the main plaza, is edged by street numbers 60, 61, 62, and 63. In Mérida, addresses are indicated as follows:

Hotel Caribe
Calle 59 #500 (x 60)

MÉRIDA

1 Banks
2 Bus Station
3 Casa de Montejo
4 Cathedral
5 Governor's Palace
6 Market
7 Regional Museum of Archaeology
8 Post and Telegraph Offices
9 Railroad Station

Calle 50
Calle 56
Calle 58
Calle 60
Calle 62
Calle 64
Calle 66
Calle 68

Calle 69
Calle 67
Calle 65
Calle 63
Calle 61
Calle 59
Calle 57
Calle 55
Calle 47
Calle 43

Paseo de Montejo

MAIN PLAZA

The "x" (by) means on or near the corner of Calle 60.

City buses cost 3.50 pesos and connect all neighborhoods *(colonias)* of the city. They run between 6:00 A.M. and 11:00 P.M.

Where to Stay

Mérida's sixteenth-century streets were designed for horse-drawn carriages and not for today's Mustangs, Broncos, and 400-horsepower engines. For maximum peace and quiet in downtown hotels (regardless of category), ask for a room in the back of the building or on one of the higher floors. Hotels are listed from the cheapest to the most expensive.

BUDGET

Hotel America *Calle 67 #500 (x 60).* Double, 300 pesos. Ceiling fans, cold water. Located on one of the busiest, noisiest market-area streets.

Casa de Huéspedes *Calle 62 #507 (x 63).* Double, 350 pesos. Ceiling fans, cold water. Old guest house with large patio.

Hotel Oviedo *Calle 62 #515 (x 65).* Double, 500 pesos. Ceiling fans, hot water, indoor parking. Rooms on street side are noisy.

Hotel María Teresa *Calle 64 #529 (x 65).* Double, 500 pesos. Ceiling fans, hot water, quiet and friendly.

Hotel San Fernando *Calle 68 (x 69, in front of the bus station).* Double, 500 pesos. Ceiling fans, hot water sometimes, noisy.

Hotel San Pablo *Calle 68 (x 69).* Double, 500 pesos.

Hospedaje *Calle 67 #550–6 (x 66).* Double, 600 pesos. Ceiling fans, hot water, quiet. One of Mérida's small, pleasant family-run guest houses.

Hotel del Parque *Calle 60 #499 (x 57).* Double, 650 pesos. Ceiling fans, hot water, room phones. Tel. 17840.

Hotel Sevilla *Calle 62 #511 (x 65).* Double, 700 pesos. Ceiling fans, hot water, patio. An old Mérida house converted into a hotel. Tel. 15258.

Hotel Londres *Calle 64 #456 (x 55).* Double, 700 pesos. Ceiling fans, hot water, very clean. Tel. 13515.

Casa Bowen (Guest House and Apartments) *Calle 66 #521 (x 65)*. Guest House, double, 450 pesos. Ceiling fans, hot water, patio. Apartments, double, 700 pesos. Bedroom, dining room with kitchenette, refrigerator, cooking utensils, bathroom with hot water, indoor parking. The children, the parents, and the grandparents all take part in running this nice, clean guest house.

Hotel San Jorge *Calle 68 (x 69, in front of bus station)*. Double, 700 pesos. Ceiling fans, hot water, modern building, noisy.

Hotel Nacional *Calle 61 #474 (x 54)*. Double, 700 pesos. Ceiling fans or air conditioning. Hot water, phone in rooms, pool. Tel. 19245.

Hotel El Caminante *Calle 64 #539 (x 65)*. Double, 700 pesos. Ceiling fans, hot water. Modern, motel-type hotel.

Gran Hotel *Calle 60 (x 59)*. Double, 700 pesos. Ceiling fans or air conditioning, hot water. Turn-of-the-century French-style architecture and décor make this hotel one of the classiest in Mérida. Tel. 17620.

Hotel Montejo *Calle 57 #507*. Double, 800 pesos. Ceiling fans or air conditioning, hot water, phone in rooms. Nice old colonial building with a beautiful patio. Tel. 14540.

Posada del Angel *Calle 67 #535*. Double, 800 pesos. Ceiling fans, hot water. Quiet, motel type.

Hotel Caribe *Calle 59 (x 60)*. Double, 800 pesos plus tax. Ceiling fans, hot water, rooftop pool, restaurant, and large patio. A central, quiet hotel. Tel. 19232.

Hotel Paris *Calle 68 #474 (x 55)*. Double, 900 pesos. Ceiling fans, hot water, indoor parking, restaurant. Tel. 38284.

Hotel Reforma *Calle 59 #508 (x 62)*. Double, 900 pesos. Ceiling fans, hot water, phone in rooms. Pool, bar, nice old building but a bit noisy. Tel. 17920.

Hotel Peninsular *Calle 58 #519 (x 65)*. Double, 1,000 pesos. Air conditioning, hot water, phone in rooms, pool, restaurant, travel agency, parking. A nice old hotel with some noisy rooms. Tel. 36996.

──────────── **MODERATE** ────────────

The following hotels have hot water, air conditioning, phone in rooms.

Hotel Colonial *Calle 62 #476.* Double, 1,400 pesos. Bar, pool. Tel. 36444.

Hotel Principe Maya *At airport.* Double, 1,100 pesos plus tax. Pool, bar, restaurant. Tel. 40411.

Hotel Cortijo *Calle 54 #365.* Double, 1,600 pesos plus tax. Parking, pool, restaurant, piano bar, car rental, large garden area. Tel. 73100.

Hotel Colón *Calle 62 #483.* Double, 1,700 pesos. Pool, restaurant, steam baths. An old colonial hotel with charm. The steam baths are open to nonguests and are reasonably priced. Tel. 34355.

Autel 59 *Calle 59 #546.* Double, 1,900 pesos plus tax. Restaurant, bar, pool, TV. Motel-type hotel. Tel. 19175.

Hotel Cayre *Calle 70 #543.* Double, 2,000 pesos. Pool, restaurant, bar, parking, gardens. Tel. 11653.

Hotel Paseo Montejo *Paseo de Montejo #482.* Double, 1,800 pesos plus tax. Restaurants, bar, pool, parking. Modern. Tel. 11641.

──────────── **DELUXE** ────────────

Hacienda Inn *Avenida Aviación, at airport.* Double, 2,200 pesos plus tax. Restaurant, bar, pool, gardens, parking. Tel. 18840.

Hotel Panamericana *Calle 59 #455 (x 52).* Double, 2,200 pesos. Restaurant, bar, pool, car rental, travel agency. The reception area is an old colonial residence, while the rooms are in a modern addition. Tel. 39444.

Hotel Mérida Misión *Calle 60 #491.* Double, 2,400 pesos plus tax. Restaurants, bar, discotheque, travel agency, pool. New but built in colonial style. One of the more appealing of the expensive hotels here. Tel. 17500.

Hotel Casa del Balam *Calle 60 #488.* Double, 2,500 plus tax. Restaurant, bar, pool. Modern and pleasant. Tel. 19474.

Hotel Montejo Palace *Paseo de Montejo 483.* Double, 2,500 pesos plus tax. Restaurants, bars, nightclub, pool. Tel. 11641.

Hotel El Castellano *Calle 57 #513.* Double, 2,700 pesos plus tax. Restaurant, bar, pool. Mérida's most modern high-rise hotel. Tel. 30100.

─────────────── **TRAILER PARK** ───────────────
Mayan's Trailer Paradise *Avenida Itzaes in front of airport entrance.* Rates not available.

━━━━━━━━ *Restaurants* ━━━━━━━━

Mérida has an ample selection of restaurants, offering Yucatecán, Mexican, and international cuisines. But remember, when in Yucatán, eat as the Yucatecáns do, and Mérida is the heartland of Yucatecán food. Be sure to treat yourself to one of Mérida's fine *comida Yucateca* restaurants. Most of them are reasonably priced.

If you are on a tight budget, try the first four restaurants on Calle 62, between 61 and 57:

El Louvre Restaurant No works of art come out of El Louvre's kitchen, but even starving artists can afford its prices. Despite its warm colas and cold soups, El Louvre has some good deals like the *comida especial* for 120 pesos. Ample menu.

Los Amigos Mostly beef and chicken dishes, approximately 120 pesos.

Restaurant Mérida Internacional This international restaurant offers mostly Yucatecán food for approximately 150 pesos.

Restaurant Maya Limited menu of Yucatecán specialties for approximately 100 pesos each to eat there or carry out.

Las Mil Tortas *Calle 62 (x 57).* Good-size pork, chicken, *longaniza,* and milanesa tortas for approximately 40 pesos each.

Ralph's Hot Dogs *Calle 62 (x 57).* Hot dogs 30, hamburgers 30, corn dogs 30 pesos. A taste of home in the heart of Mérida.

El Chino *Calle 62 (x 61).* *Salbutes* 15, *panuchos* 15, tostadas 15, tortas 20 pesos.

Lonchería Mérida *Calle 62 (x 61).* *Salbutes* 15, *panuchos* 15, tostadas 15, tortas 40 pesos.

Restaurant Nichte-Ha *North side of main plaza, sign reads* Comida Yucateca *(Yucatecán food).* Ample menu with most dishes approximately 150 pesos.

Restaurant Leo *Paseo de Montejo and Calle 35.* Mexican food. Grilled pork and beef tacos, *quesadillas,* and cheese fondues. Reasonably priced and very popular.

Restaurant Yu Liang's *Paseo de Montejo #435 (inside Edificio Cristal).* Ample menu of Chinese food for approximately 250 pesos.

Restaurant La Isla de Hawai *Calle 60 #511.* A popular seafood restaurant with an ample menu and reasonable prices.

Restaurant Expresso *Calle 60 (x 59).* Assorted menu of beef, chicken, and seafood dishes for approximately 150 pesos a plate. Good coffee and good service.

Restaurant Les Balcóns *Calle 60 #497, second floor.* Vegetarian food. Vegetarian pizza, 150 pesos small size, 230 pesos large size. Soups, salads, and other vegetarian dishes. Also has about 10 beef and chicken dishes.

Las Monjas *Calle 64 #509 (x 63).* Assorted menu of meat, chicken, and fish dishes. Filet mignon with mushrooms 250, *carne à la Tampiqueña* 250, *pollo pibil* 130, fish fillets prepared in various styles 140 pesos a dish. Patio dining.

Restaurant Los Almendras *Calle 59 #434 (x 50A).* One of the best Yucatecán restaurants in the peninsula. Very reasonably priced.

Restaurant Soberanis *Calle 60 #501 (x 63).* This is the peninsula's sovereign of seafoods. The menu consists of over 60 seafood dishes costing approximately 150 pesos each.

Restaurant El Mesón del Mestizo *Calle 55 (x 60), Parque Santa Lucia.* Mex-Yuca-American. Yucatecán dishes approximately 160 pesos, American-style steaks—sirloin, T-bone, pepper steak—

approximately 300, seafood plates approximately 200 pesos. Pleasant outdoor restaurant.

Restaurant La Carreta   *Calle 62 (x 59)*. Mixed menu. Beef, pork, chicken, and seafood dishes. American-style steaks approximately 300 pesos. Wine by the glass.

Restaurant El Ofir de Ali   *Calle 60 (x 55)*. Arab food. Kibbeh (lamb cooked with mint) 160, lamb brochette 300, tabouleh 90 pesos. Small, cozy, and quiet.

Restaurant Colón   *Calle 62 #487 (x 57)*. French-international cuisine. House specialties are champagne chicken 300, steak flambé 450, châteaubriand with béarnaise sauce 600 pesos. Wine list. The setting is old, hard to define, but definitely intriguing. Tel. 34355.

Restaurant La Casona   *Calle 60 #434 (x 47)*. Italian food at its best with homemade pasta for less than 230 pesos. Most meat and seafood dishes under 300 pesos. Ample list of Mexican and imported wines. Tel. 38348.

I did not personally visit the following restaurants, but they have a good reputation among Mérida's connoisseurs.

Los Pájaros   *Calle 30 and Avenida Cupules*. Yucatecán food. Tel. 51735.

El Tío Ricardo   *Calle 8 #201 (x 23)*. American-style steaks. Tel. 21000.

Le Gourmet   *Avenida Perez Ponce #109*. Creole cuisine. Tel. 71970.

Alberto's Continental Patio   *Calle 64 (x 57)*. International and Lebanese cuisine. Tel. 12298.

Restaurant Las Almejas   *Calle 60 #329*. Seafood. Tel. 77288.

Nightlife

If your budget and energy allow it, Mérida has enough nightlife activities to keep you going until the early hours of the morning. The **Restaurant Jardín** at the Hotel Mérida Misión (Calle 60 #491) presents a show every night and dinner at 8:30 and 9:30 P.M. The dinner consists of fruit cocktail, soup, main dish, dessert, coffee, and two drinks. The show is a mosaic of Mayan and Yucatecán dances. The price for dinner, show, and two drinks is 350 pesos per person and for the show only 200 pesos with one drink included. For reservations call 39500.

A different kind of show is presented by the **Restaurant Mariachi's Hacienda** (Calle 60 #466, x 53), where for the price of dinner or a couple of drinks you can watch mariachis playing the traditional songs of central Mexico. Most fish and chicken dishes cost approximately 250 pesos. Meat dishes are more expensive, costing between 350 and 400 pesos. The house specialties are enchiladas Suizas 225, chiles rellenos 225, and enchiladas rojas 230 pesos. Mixed drinks with Mexican liquors cost 100 pesos and 120 pesos with imported liquors. Open nightly until 2:00 A.M. For reservations call 10183.

Fads don't fade away so quickly in Mexico, and disco music and discos are still very popular. **Le Tuch** at the Hotel Mérida Misión offers dancing music by a popular Mérida group. The cover charge is 50 pesos Monday through Wednesday and 100 pesos Thursday through Saturday. There is a three-drink minimum.

Not far from Le Tuch is **Pancho Villa's Follies** (at Calle 59, x 62) where you can dine, drink, and dance all under the same roof. A dinner of red snapper Veracruzana costs approximately 250 pesos, mixed drinks are 120 pesos, and the canned disco music is yours for the dancing.

For additional nightlife activities check with desk clerks and local tourist publications for current hot spots and shows. Also keep in mind that the better hotels usually offer some type of entertainment in their restaurants and bars.

For the cheapest and simplest nightlife you need only walk on the downtown streets and join the locals for a stroll around the main plaza. Paseo de Montejo, with its wide, tree-studded sidewalks, restaurants, and shops, is another favorite strolling area of the Méridans.

In the main plaza on Sunday nights, the city's band plays a potpourri of Mexican, American, and other international hits, often dedicated to their country of origin.

For a taste of the folklore, dances, and songs of Yucatán, be sure to go to tiny **Parque de Santa Lucia** (Calle 60, x 55) where *noches de serenata* are presented every Thursday night at 8:00 P.M.

Tours

Sight-seeing in Mérida can be done in one of three ways:

1. Take a guided tour through one of the local travel agencies. These tours include the city's main streets, colonial buildings, and monuments. Some also include the market.

2. Take a *calesa* (horse-drawn carriage) tour, costing 300 pesos for a maximum of four people. Calesa tours start at Calle 60 and go past Parques Hidalgo, Santa Lucia, and Santa Ana, then take Paseo de Montejo as far as the monument to the history of Mexico, before returning to the point of departure. There are two calesa stands downtown at the corners of Calle 59 (x 60) and 61 (x 60).

3. Explore the sights by walking or taking city buses (fare 5.50 pesos).

The Governor's Palace *(Casa de los Gobernadores)* is located on the northern side of the main plaza. It was finished in 1872 and is the seat of Yucatán State's government.

Distributed over its ground and second floors are a series of murals depicting various aspects of Mexican, Yucatecán, and Mayan history. On the second floor, facing the main plaza, is the Salón de la Historia with 17 large paintings dealing with class struggle, Mayan slavery, and other chapters of Yucatecán history. All the paintings were done by Yucatecán painter Fernando Castro Pacheco between 1971 and 1978.

The Cathedral is located on the eastern side of the main plaza (Plaza Mayor). The construction of this fortresslike church was started in 1561 and was not finished until 1598.

Casa de Montejo is located on the southern side of the main plaza and was the residence of Francisco Montejo, Mérida's founder. Recently Casa de Montejo was remodeled and turned into bank offices, but it can still be visited from 4:00 to 6:00 P.M.

Museo Regional de Arqueología *Paseo de Montejo and Calle 43.* The Regional Museum of Archaeology is an excellent place to visit before you tour the peninsula's numerous ruin sites. The museum consists of seven large rooms with well-mounted exhibits on, for example, the geological history of the Yucatán Peninsula, the Olmecs, Toltecs, and other cultures related to the Mayans. Jewelry, musical instruments, funeral practices, and many other aspects of

Mayan life are on display. All explanations are in Spanish, but Señor Manuel Zavala, at the museum's entrance, offers guided tours in English for 150 pesos an hour. Open 9:00 A.M. to 8:00 P.M. Closed Monday.

Parque de las Américas *Avenida Colón.* This park is dedicated to the nations of the American continent with small monuments erected in honor of each individual country.

Mérida's attractive **main plaza** is flanked by streets 60, 61, 62, and 63.

Paseo de Montejo is a wide, tree-lined avenue with the city's most elegant mansions. Many of them were built at the turn of the century in French style. There are plenty of restaurants, shops, travel agencies, hotels, and banks on Paseo de Montejo.

Mercado *Calle 65 (x 56).* Mérida's market is the largest and most interesting one in the Yucatán Peninsula, covering several of the city's downtown blocks. Vegetables, fruit, meat, hardware, kitchenware, and just about everything under the Mayan sun are sold.

Shopping

There are many handcraft stores throughout Mérida's downtown streets. The market, however, has a large concentration of them. On the corner of Calle 60 (x 65), there is a group of about 20 stands selling mostly regional clothes.

A few blocks from here, at the crossing of Calle 67 (x 56A), right in the heart of the market, the Handcraft Bazaar is located. As you go up the ramp in front of Calle 67 there are two buildings to your right and left. Both of them have a large number of stands with handcrafts from all over Mexico. You will find ceramic plates, bowls, vases, pots, and figurines, leather belts, purses and coats, lacquered bowls and platters, silver jewelry, and many more things.

The best shopping bargains, though, are usually the crafts produced in the peninsula, such as *guayaberas, huipiles,* conch shells with Mayan-motif etchings, black coral, hammocks, and Panama hats (which incidentally are made in neighboring Campeche State and not in Panama).

Bargaining is an acceptable way of shopping in market handcraft shops. Don't be shy about trying it; you can only gain by doing so.

Hammocks

Before I went to Tixkokob I was a bit confused about how to choose a good hammock. By the time I left there, I was totally confused.

I hope the following hints will help you more than confuse you in choosing a good hammock at a good price.

1. The hammock's main body should be at least 5 feet 8 inches in length.

2. The weave of the main body should be tight enough that you cannot easily put a finger through it when the hammock is not stretched.

3. End strings are counted in pairs. Each pair should hold a minimum of 3 loops of the main body.

4. The edge should have up to 30 tightly weaved, parallel strings. A wide edge is essential to keep you from falling off the hammock and to keep its shape.

5. A hammock should have a certain number of double end strings according to its size.

Size	Pairs of End Strings	Price Range at Tixkokob (Pesos)
Individual	90 to 120	250 to 350
Medium	120 to 150	350 to 450
Matrimonial	150 to 170	450 to 550
Family	170 to 280	550 to 1000

DAY TRIPS FROM MÉRIDA

Mérida's travel agencies offer guided tours to the ruins of Chichén Itzá, Uxmal, Kabáh, Dzibilchaltún, the caves of Loltun, and also a city tour. The price of guided tours includes transportation, English-speaking guides, and admission to the ruins. Lunch is extra. The price of tours varies greatly from one travel agency to another. For example, Martinez Yucatán Travel Service offers a city tour for 200 pesos, while one of its competitors charges 360 pesos for the same tour. Before buying your tour ticket, shop around and compare to see if higher prices come with better services.

Travel agencies *(agencias de viajes)* can be found in the better hotels and in the main streets of downtown Mérida. The following is a partial list of Mérida's travel agencies:

Aeroexpress	Tel. 11641
Rutas del Mayab	19984
Barbachano Travel	39444
Colón Travel Bureau	17980
Martinez Travel	76574
Aviomar	30439
Yucatán Caribe	10305
Bojorquez	34893
Viajes el Castellano	30100
Wagon-Lits Mexicana	12032

The **ruins of Dzibilchaltún and Progreso** are a short 66-km (41-mile) day trip combining a visit to the ruins of Dzibilchaltún and the beach at Progreso and/or other neighboring beaches.

Progreso is Yucatán State's most important port and Mérida's most popular beach. It is unfair to compare, but as a beach, Progreso lacks the beautiful turquoise color and clarity of the water on the Caribbean side of the Yucatán Peninsula. But Progreso nonetheless has what most beach lovers look for: warm water, plenty of sunshine, and soft, caressing sand. Shell collectors should bring a truck, as shells here can be picked by the bushel.

Other smaller beaches not far from Progreso are Chiczulub, 7 km to the east, and Chelem and Chuburna, 11 and 18 km respectively to the west.

Getting There

Car Take Calle 60 at the main square and follow Progreso signs. The Dzibilchaltún Road junction is located at km 15 on the Progreso Highway. The ruins are 4.5 km from here.

Bus Take the bus at the Progreso bus station, Calle 66 (x 65). There are buses to and from Progreso every 30 minutes. Buses to Dzibilchaltún leave at 7:15 A.M., noon, and 4:15 P.M. Buses returning to Mérida leave at 8:15 A.M., 1:00 P.M., and 5:15 P.M.

Only Mayan gods know how many of the ruins' stones at Dzibil-chaltún have been used to build churches, haciendas, and mansions. All that remains today at Dzibilchaltún are a few scattered ruins and a sixteenth-century Catholic chapel. Archaeologically, the ruins of Dzibilchaltún are as important and interesting as any other, but because of their proximity to Mérida, they have been a bit overrated as a tourist attraction. So don't come here expecting to find numerous and magnificent Mayan pyramids and temples because you might just ruin your day (particularly if you came by bus).

Admission: 5 pesos weekdays and 3 pesos Sundays. Open 8:00 A.M. to 5:00 P.M.

Izamal The round trip from Mérida to Izamal is 180 km (111 miles). The main sights there are the Great Pyramid of Kinich Kakmo and the former Convent and Church of San Francisco, which has the biggest atrium in Mexico.

Getting There

Car Take the Chichén Itzá–Cancún Highway to the town of Hoctún, 47 km (29 miles) east of Mérida. At Hoctún's main plaza, take the paved road on your left to Kimbila-Citilcum, 13 km (8 miles). From Citilcum it is only 11 km (7 miles) to Izamal.

Bus There are several daily departures from Mérida's central bus station to Izamal.

Izamal is located 90 km (56 miles) east of Mérida and has a population of approximately 25,000 inhabitants. Its main source of income is agriculture, particularly henequen.

The name of the city derives from the Mayan high priest Itzamná, who according to legend is buried here. Izamal is also known as the "Yellow City," because most of the houses and buildings in this colonial city are painted yellow.

One of the main attractions at Izamal is the Pyramid of Kinich Kakmo, one of the largest in the Yucatán Peninsula. This pyramid has been partly reconstructed and its height and the size of its base are of impressive proportions. From the top of the pyramid, there is an excellent view of the city, the henequen plantations, and the rest of Izamal's attractions: the Convent, Church, and atrium of San Francisco.

Tixkokob and the Ruins of Ake   The round trip to Tixkokob and Ake is only 60 km (37 miles). Tixkokob is the main hammock-making town in the Yucatán Peninsula, while Ake is an interesting juxtaposition of a turn-of-the-century henequen hacienda built within the site of the Mayan ruins of the same name.

━━━━━━━━━━━━━━━ *Getting There* ━━━━━━━━━━━━━━━

Car   Take the Chichén Itzá–Cancún Highway as far as the Y junction on the outskirts of Mérida. The right-hand side of the Y goes to Chichén Itźa and Cancún and the left one to Tixkokob and Motul. There are road signs to these destinations, but keep a sharp eye out for them. The junction for the ruins of Ake is on the east end of Calle 21 (the main street) at Tixkokob.

Bus   There are frequent bus departures from the Central de Autobuses to Tixkokob, but from here to the ruins of Ake there is only one bus, leaving at approximately 11:00 A.M.

The people of Tixkokob work hard so that you and I may loaf around in one of the fine hammocks made here. It takes about 40 continuous hours of tedious work to make an individual-size hammock and almost three times as long to make a gigantic family-size one big enough for Mama, Papa, and a couple of the kids.

But as I found out during my recent two-day visit here, few people in town are engaged solely in the making of hammocks for a living. I was told by one of the older women in the village that the women make the hammocks, but it takes them about three weeks to finish one because they weave them in their spare time. Spare time, I should add, is the time left between raising children, cleaning house, cooking, doing errands, shopping, etc. In other towns on the peninsula, spare time is spent lying in hammocks; here it is spent weaving them.

In Tixkokob you can buy your hammock from weavers or hammock dealers. Weavers can be found easily. Walk around the town's streets, Calle 21, for example, and look inside any open door. (People here leave their doors open either for sunlight and air circulation or to let it be known that they weave hammocks.) Stop where you see a hammock loom, greet the weaver, or if no one is in sight, knock and say *"Buenos Días."*

The rest is pretty much up to your language and bargaining abilities and whether or not the weaver has spare hammocks to sell. Often the hammocks they are weaving are already sold, but in this case, most weavers are more than willing to refer you to their sister, cousin, niece, or mother-in-law who "happens to have precisely the hammock you are looking for."

Two of the countless weavers in Tixkokob are Señorita Virginia Lara, Calle 21 #60, and Señor René Guerra, Calle 18 #108 (by the railroad station).

Hammock dealers usually have an ample stock of hammock sizes and prices and are the easiest, quickest source for buying a hammock if you don't have the time to shop around and look for weavers. Some of the hammock merchants in Tixkokob are Familia Ancona, Calle 21 #86; Familia González, Calle 16 #88; Familia Pat Pasos, Calle 15 #79; Tienda el Gallo, Calle 21 #83; and Manuel Pech, Calle 21 #136.

Manuel Pech is a Mayan weaver turned dealer, and he has a most amazing technical hammock-weaving English vocabulary. If he is not here resting in hammocks that he is testing, you will find him selling them in Isla Mujeres or Cancún.

The Yucatán Peninsula has hundreds of hidden Mayan ruin sites, and in many cases entire Mayan cities may be found within the boundaries of cattle ranches and henequen plantations. Considering this, it is not too farfetched to think of a local rancher saying to his friends, "Come visit me sometime and we will have lunch on top of my Mayan pyramid."

The ruins of **Ake** are one such hidden Mayan ruin site. Scattered around several square miles of the hacienda's henequen plantations are several large mounds of dirt and stones—remnants of Mayan buildings. Chances are, however, that most of the stones that form the hacienda's buildings came from those mounds, and if this is the case, restoration of the ruins is impossible.

There are, however, three Mayan buildings that are still in fair condition, and all are incongruously blended with the hacienda's house, church, corrals, and the small sisal-rope plant operating there. The main concentration of ruins is on the right-hand corner of the hacienda as you face it. A small, steep pyramid is located on the left-hand side.

A to Z

AIRLINES

Aeromexico *Main office: Calle 60 (x 57).* Tel 36644. Airport: Tel. 11556.

Continental Airlines Airport: Tel. 36921.

Eastern Airlines Airport: Tel. 33811.

Mexicana *Main office: Calle 58 #500.* Tel. 12780, 12755. Airport: Tel. 36986, 38602.

United Airlines Airport: Tel. 31899.

AIRPORT

Mérida's airport building is about the size of a small city block and all its services are found within easy walking distance. Among the services you will find here are long-distance and local phones, telegraph and post offices, car rental agencies, a restaurant and a bar, several craft shops, and a money exchange booth (open 8:00 A.M. to 8:00 P.M.). The exchange booth will give you less than the official rate. Change only what you will need until you can go to a bank.

Taxis charge 250 pesos to take you downtown or 100 pesos per person in group taxis. City buses stop on the right-hand side, as you exit the terminal, and run every 15 minutes between 7:00 A.M. and 9:00 P.M. These buses wind around town a bit but will ultimately take you to Calle 67 (x 62) downtown. To go to the airport, take the same bus (79 Aviación). The fare is 5.50 pesos.

Remember to save some money at the end of your trip for the airport tax. The international departure tax is 300 pesos and the national departure tax is 100 pesos.

BANKS

Banking hours are 9:00 A.M. to 1:30 P.M. and there is no shortage of banks in Mérida. There are five banks on Calle 65, downtown, between Calles 60 and 62, one block south of the main plaza.

BUS STATION

Mérida's Central de Autobuses is located on the corner of Calle 68 (x 69). There is a bank and a long-distance telephone office there.

———————————— **CAR RENTALS** ————————————

Day rental rates are standard for most cars in most rental agencies. The first thing to do in agencies that offer below-average rates is to ask what year the car is. If it is a late model, then you have a deal. Collision damage and personal insurance is 250 pesos, and tax is 15 percent of the total amount.

Volkswagen sedans, Rabbits, and vans are the most economical cars, but most American cars are also available.

There are several car rental agencies at the Mérida airport. The following is a list of car rental agencies and their main office phone numbers:

Avis	Tel. 14599
Budget	18223
Cosmopolitan	10548
Ford	36196
Hertz	18020
Holiday	19644
Max	10808
Napeca	36002
National	78277
Quick	34097
Volkswagen Rent	18128
Yucatán Rent	10009

———————————— **CONSULATES** ————————————

American Consulate   *Paseo de Montejo 453.* Tel. 77011.

British Consulate   *Calle 58 #450.* Tel. 16794.

Canadian Consulate   *Fraccionamiento Campestre IF 249 (x 36).* Tel. 70460.

———————————— **JUGOS** ————————————

Méridans are very fond of fresh fruit juices *(jugos),* fruit cocktails *(cocteles de fruta),* and fruit drinks *(licuados).* As you walk around the city's streets you will see signs reading *Jugos y Licuados.* Go into one of these places and you will discover what looks like a shooting gallery of fruit. On the shelves are row upon row of cantaloupes, bananas, watermelons, papayas, oranges, pineapples, and other fruits that you might not know, like *mameys* and *guanábanas.*

Don't be afraid, the *jugo* places keep things pretty clean and use purified water and pasteurized milk. Draw out your wallet and shoot for your choice of *jugo, licuado,* or *coctel de fruta.* Most *jugos* cost approximately 40 pesos, *licuados* 40 pesos, and fruit cocktails 60 pesos.

POST OFFICE

The post office is located at Calle 65 (x 56) near the market area. Open 9:00 A.M. to 7:00 P.M. Monday through Friday and 9:00 A.M. to 1:00 P.M. Saturday.

TAXIS

Hail a taxi on the street or call one at the following numbers: 12500, 12200, and 12133. For late-night service, call 12300 or 11221. The rates are 80 pesos within Mérida's downtown area and 200 pesos to the airport.

TELEGRAPH OFFICE

Same address and hours as the post office.

TOURIST INFORMATION

Yucatán State's Tourist Department operates a one-man bilingual information booth outside the Governor's Palace, Calle 60 (x 61), open from 10:00 A.M. to 4:00 P.M. Monday through Friday and 10:00 A.M. to 2:00 P.M. Saturday. There is also an information booth at the airport that is open during the same hours. In both booths, most tourist information is transmitted orally. Maps and pamphlets are scarce.

Uxmal

Uxmal was founded in the sixth century A.D., but most of its main buildings were erected between the seventh and tenth centuries. Because of the proportions and beauty of its buildings, Uxmal is the most outstanding Mayan city in the Yucatán Peninsula.

Architecturally, Uxmal belongs to the Mayan Puuc style, and unlike Chichén Itzá, its buildings show little or none of the Toltec influence. The Puuc style of architecture is characterized by intricate, geometrical relief work running the length of the building, executed on the facade at a level immediately above the doorways. Between entryways the walls are without decoration. (Admission: 15 pesos, 10 pesos on holidays).

Getting There

Bus There are several direct bus runs from the Mérida bus station. See A to Z, Mérida.

Car From Mérida, take Highway 180 toward Campeche. At Umán, 17 km (10 miles) from Mérida, take the highway to Muna, 62 km (38 miles) south. From Muna's main plaza it's 16 km (10 miles) to Uxmal.

The Temple of the Magician is an unusual cone-shaped pyramid consisting of several superimposed structures. It is also called the Temple of the Dwarf, after a former ruler of Uxmal who was a dwarf.

The Quadrangle of the Nuns is a group of four large buildings built around a central courtyard. They are richly decorated with carvings of Chac, the rain god, undulating serpents, and many other motifs.

The Palace of the Governors is a spectacular building, and along with those of the Quadrangle of the Nuns, is among the finest examples of Puuc architecture—and among the most beautiful of Mayan buildings.

The House of the Turtles (Casa de las Tortugas), a small building located north of the Palace of the Governors, derives its name from the turtle sculptures located in its upper half.

Where to Stay

MODERATE

Hotel Villas Arqueológicas Double, 2,000 pesos. Restaurant, bar, and pool.

Hotel Misión Uxmal Double, 2,300 pesos. Restaurant, bar, and pool.

DELUXE

Hotel Hacienda Uxmal Double, 2,600 pesos. Restaurant, bar, and pool.

There are a couple of budget hotels and restaurants at Muna, 10 miles north of Uxmal.

Chichén Itzá

The original constructions of Chichén Itzá, the Nunnery, the Akab Dzid, the Observatory, and the Deer House, among others, are of the Puuc, or classic, Mayan style, and may date back to the fourth century A.D. Mysteriously, Chichén Itzá was abandoned in the seventh century. Between the ninth and fourteenth centuries, the Itzás, a displaced Toltec group from central Mexico, blended in with the Mayans and brought about an architectural and cultural rebirth of Chichén Itzá. Among other elements, the Itzás introduced human sacrifice and the worship of Quetzalcoatl, translated in the Mayan language as Kukulkán.

Just as the Spanish conquerors destroyed the Mayan pyramids and temples to build their own churches and convents, the Itzás rebuilt some Mayan structures to suit their own religious beliefs. The Temple of Kukulkán, for example, was built by the Itzás over a smaller Mayan pyramid. Other constructions, like the Temple of the Bearded Man and the Great Ball Court, were added to Chichén Itzá by the Itzás.

Chichén Itzá is a large site, with about 50 buildings of various sizes. The ruins are divided into Old Chichén, south of the highway, and New Chichén, north of it. The following are some of the most outstanding structures at Chichén Itzá.

Getting There

Bus Through buses from Mérida and Cancún service Chichén Itzá about every 30 minutes.

Car Chichén Itzá is 120 km (74 miles) east of Mérida on the Mérida–Puerto Juárez Highway.

NEW CHICHÉN

El Castillo   The Castle, or the Temple of Kukulkán, is one of the largest pyramids found on the peninsula. Each one of its four sides has a steep stairway with 91 steps.

Temple of the Warriors is also known as the Temple of the Thousand Columns. Each one of the columns has carvings of warriors.

The Sacred Well is the *cenote* where human sacrifices were made to Chac, the rain god.

Tzompantli is a platform with carvings of human skulls. It is believed that the skulls of captured chieftains were displayed here.

Temple of the Jaguars is at the entrance to the Ball Court and has some beautiful carvings of warriors and jaguars.

The Ball Court at Chichén Itzá is the largest ball court in the Yucatán Peninsula. It is 545 feet long and 225 feet wide. The game of pok-a-tok was played here, with a rubber ball that had to be passed through the stone rings on the court's walls.

The Temple of the Bearded Man is a small temple located on the north end of the Ball Court, and it was probably from there that the city's leaders watched the ball game.

OLD CHICHÉN

The Observatory consists of superimposed platforms, with a large round tower built on top of them. This tower is the observatory proper and was used for astronomical studies.

The Church is a tall rectangular building located to the right side of the observatory. It belongs to the Puuc architectural style.

The Nunnery is a long rectangular complex with many built-in chambers, which the Spanish thought were nuns' cells.

Where to Stay

The hotels right at the ruins of Chichén Itzá, Hacienda Chichén and Mayaland, are in the deluxe range and have double rooms for approximately 3,000 pesos a night. The tiny town of Pisté, one mile west of the ruins, has the following places to stay.

BUDGET

Piramide Inn Trailer Park   Cars 50 pesos plus 50 pesos per person. Camping space, hot showers, clean WCs. Very little shade.

Posada Novelo   Double, 450 pesos. Fans and cold water.

―――――――――――― **MODERATE** ――――――――――――

Piramide Inn   Double, 1,000 pesos. Air conditioning, hot water, pool, restaurant.

―――――――――――― **DELUXE** ――――――――――――

Hotel Misión   Double, 2,000 pesos. Air conditioning, pool.

―――――――――――― **VALLADOLID** ――――――――――――

Valladolid is a city of some 30,000 inhabitants located 41 km (25 miles) east of Chichén Itzá. There are 10 hotels in town, all in the budget range (below 1,000 pesos). Some of them are nice and would be considered deluxe in Cancún and Cozumel. All of them are located near the main plaza.

―――――――――――― **BUDGET** ――――――――――――

Hotel Ma Guadalupe   Double, 500 pesos.

Hotel San Clemente   Double, 500 pesos.

Hotel Zaci   Double, 500 pesos.

Hotel El Mesón del Marques   Double, 700 pesos.

Restaurants

There are no restaurants right at the ruins. The town of Pisté has eight, most of which serve dishes for approximately 200 pesos. Valladolid also has several restaurants, most offering meals below 200 pesos. El Bazar, at the main plaza, is a concentration of clean food stands serving typical Yucatecán dishes. Meals cost under 150 pesos; open only for dinner.

San Felipe

San Felipe is a charming little town located at the mouth of the Río Lagartos estuary. In the ten square blocks or so that make up the entire town, you will find a church, a movie house, a small restaurant, and a few stores. With its narrow streets and wooden houses, San Felipe resembles its neighbor, Río Lagartos. (Like Río Lagartos, San Felipe has its share of mosquitoes.) But perhaps because it is smaller and more isolated, it is slower paced and seems friendlier and cozier.

Located on the edges of Yucatán State's richest cattle country and the fish-rich Caribbean waters, San Felipe's 300 inhabitants are an unusual combination of cowboys and fishermen. As you walk through the town's streets you may spot a cowboy on horseback sporting American cowboy hat and boots, or a fisherman repairing a net that hangs from the tile roof of his house.

San Felipe is an ideal spot to escape tourists completely. What's more, if you're interested in getting to know the people and the language of Mexico, this is a great little town in which to soak up some culture and sun. There is no bank, telegraph, telephone, or post office in San Felipe. Río Lagartos is the closest town with services.

Getting There

Car   Take Highway 295 at Valladolid to Tizimín, then continue on to Río Lagartos. The turnoff for San Felipe is at km 101, 3 kilometers from Río Lagartos. The 10-kilometer (6-mile) road to San Felipe is a one-lane paved road with passing shoulders every kilometer. The outgoing vehicles, closest to the passing shoulder, must pull off the road to allow incoming vehicles to pass. There is no gas station in San Felipe.

Bus There are no direct buses from Valladolid to San Felipe. From the Valladolid Central Bus Station, buses for Tizimín leave every two hours. From Tizimín, there are two daily buses to San Felipe, at 6:00 A.M. and 1:30 P.M. The bus fare from Valladolid to San Felipe is 100 pesos.

Where to Stay

San Felipe doesn't have a hotel. The closest thing to it are the rooms for rent located above the Cinema Marrufo, the local movie house. These rooms are seldom rented and you might find yourself sweeping the floor and making the bed as you move in. A double room costs 150 pesos a day and you must share a bathroom and shower. For information about the rooms, ask at La Herradura grocery store, one block from the pier.

Houses can also be rented at La Herradura for 150 pesos a day for up to four people. They have little or no furniture, a bathroom, cement floors, and wooden walls and roofs. Ask around for better, furnished houses *(casas con muebles)*.

Restaurants

Restaurant El Payaso *one block east of La Herradura.* This is the only restaurant in town. The menu consists of fried fish, fish soup, ceviche, and a few other seafood items. A meal here costs less than 150 pesos.

Beaches and Activities

San Felipe's beach can be reached by a short boat ride across the estuary, which separates the mainland from the Río Lagartos Peninsula. Although there is no regular boat service to the beach, arrangements for a round trip can be made with local fishing-boat owners who can be found at the town's small concrete pier. The cost is 30 pesos per person for the round trip.

There is no refreshment stand at the beach, so take water and food with you. (For more information on this beach see Beach Hiking/Camping, Río Lagartos, page 54.)

Río Lagartos

Río Lagartos ("Alligator River") gets its name from the once-abundant population of alligators found in the area's swamps. Unfortunately, the lack of ecological awareness and protection laws has left only a few alligators in the area.

The town's multicolored wooden houses, built on narrow streets, give it a personality and charm of its own. The small triangular plaza in the center of town is, as in most towns throughout Mexico, the political, social, cultural, and religious center of the community. On one side of the plaza is the town's Catholic church; on the other side is the city hall.

———— *Getting There* ————

Car Take Highway 295 at Valladolid to Tizimín, then continue on to Río Lagartos. The total distance is 103 km (64 miles) over a paved two-lane road with no shoulders. There are Pemex stations at Valladolid, Tizimín, and Río Lagartos.

Bus There are no direct buses from Valladolid to Río Lagartos. From the Valladolid Central de Autobuses, buses leave at 7:00, 9:30, and 11:00 A.M., noon, and 1:30 and 4:30 P.M. The fare is 50 pesos. With proper connections, total bus-riding time from Valladolid to Río Lagartos is 2 hours. Tizimín is a very pleasant place, and if you have to wait a couple of hours for your bus, you might want to take a walk around town. The bus station is only 3 blocks away from the main plaza.

Where to Stay

BUDGET

Hotel Nefertiti. Located on the town's waterfront, the Nefertiti is the only hotel in town. The rate is 600 pesos for a double. All rooms have ceiling fans and individual bathrooms with hot and cold water. The second-floor rooms, facing north, have a view of the estuary.

Restaurants

Restaurant Nefertiti. *Hotel Nefertiti.* This is the town's restaurant, bar, and discotheque. The décor of fluorescent sea stars, fish, and flamingos is enough to make you want to eat with your eyes closed. The food, though, is much better than the décor, the menu consisting mainly of seafood dishes. Lunch and dinner dishes cost approximately 100 pesos.

Restaurant Santiaguito *Main Plaza.* If you are on a budget and have a medium-size sense of humor, you can have an inexpensive (120 pesos) and fair meal here. The restaurant's menu depends on the availability of fish, eggs, tortillas, etc. in the nearby stores.

The first time I ate here, I asked the owner if he had fried fish. "*Sí*, of course," he said. As I sat down I saw a child running out the door with an empty plate. In no time he was back with a pan-sized raw fish. When I was served the cooked fish, I asked for tortillas and once again the kid made a dash out the door. A few minutes later, hot steaming tortillas landed on my table. I hesitated for a while and finally I decided to order a beer, and sure enough, zoom!—the kid runs to the store across from the restaurant. By then, realizing that the little runner was burning as many calories as I was eating, I felt guilty, and when he came back I handed him a 10-peso coin to thank him for his help.

Beaches and Activities

The beach of Río Lagartos is located on the north side of the Río Lagartos Peninsula and is accessible only by boat. The Nefertiti Hotel has a beach shuttle boat that runs by arrangement. The boat rental is 100 pesos round trip for two passengers. The boat operator will drop you off at the beach and will return for you at the hour you indicate.

As you cross the estuary and go through the canal you will have a chance to see large numbers of cormorants, plovers, pelicans, herons, and many other birds.

When you arrive at the beach, the boat will drop you off on the west side of the canal. There is an almost constant breeze and about one foot of surf. The beach slope is steep in some stretches, with water coming up to waist level at about 3 yards from the surf line.

There is no cover from the sun anywhere on this hot beach. If you don't have a good tan base, the wind and the sun will burn you badly before you even realize it. Make sure to take appropriate clothing with you to cover yourself *before* you have had enough sun. Bring your own food and water as there are none available here.

BIRD-WATCHING

Even if you aren't a bird-watching enthusiast, the Flamingo Sanctuary is a rare and beautiful sight and enough reason for a trip to Río Lagartos.

Thousands of pink flamingos live and raise their offspring in the low-water areas east of Río Lagartos. The flamingos' cone-shaped nests, built out of mud and sticks, are raised up to a foot above the ground. Flamingos are impressive birds. An adult bird stands 5 feet high and has a wingspan of 5 feet. When you see one of these tall, graceful birds, it is hard to believe that it only weighs 7 pounds.

As your boat approaches the shallow banks where they feed, you look into the horizon and you might think to yourself, "I must be getting heatstroke, I'm seeing pink." Don't worry, you are not getting heatstroke, but you are for sure seeing pink.

Standing on the banks of the lagoon, a couple of miles ahead of you, a flock of some 3,000 flamingos colors the horizon in flaming red and pink. By the way, the word *flamingo* comes from the Spanish *flamenco*, literally meaning "flaming." Then, as the boat gets closer, the whole flock takes off into the sky, creating the effect of a bright red sunset that would turn the sun green with envy. They circle overhead a couple of times in a display of sound and color and then land, always keeping a distance of some 300 yards from their admirers.

Unless you have a shallow-bottom boat, the only way to reach the flamingo viewing area is through the 2-hour tour conducted by the Nefertiti Hotel in Río Lagartos. The tour price is 75 pesos per person and requires a minimum of four people. Make arrangements for your tour the night before you plan to go.

This tour, however, is much too short for such a beautiful and rare sight. The fellow who conducts it turns the boat around almost the minute you have sighted the flamingos. Before you go on the tour, make clear to him that you did not come all the way to Río Lagartos to see the flamingos for 2 minutes. The man is reasonable, but he has seen enough flamingos to have pink dreams.

If you have your own boat, here is how to get to the flamingo viewing area: take the dirt road 3.5 km (2 miles) south of Río Lagartos, to Las Coloradas, 14 km (8.7 miles) from Río Lagartos. From the eastern edge of Las Coloradas, it is 7.5 km (4.6 miles) to a small wooden pier marked *La Villa. Embarcadero Flamencos.* The flamingo viewing area is about a 10-minute boat ride south of the pier. The water is 2 to 3 feet deep and even shallower as you approach the flamingo area. Turn off your motor when you are about 400 yards from the flamingos and then row toward them.

With its marshes, swamps, lagoons, and mud flats, Río Lagartos is a paradise for water birds and bird-watchers. But the very conditions that make the area ideal for water birds make it difficult for bird-watchers to have access to the birds. There are, however, other areas of easy access where birds can be seen. Look for snowy egrets, great white herons, reddish egrets, black-necked stilts, white ibis, and other birds along the road to the *cenote* on the eastern side of town; the swamp area on the edges of the highway to Tizimín, a mile from the center of town; and the sand banks on the Río Lagartos Canal, as you go to the beach. The best time for bird-watching in these spots is early in the morning.

CAMPING

There is a beautiful *cenote* three-quarters of a mile east of the Nefertiti Hotel, along the water. The *cenote* is surrounded by a large dirt parking area ideal for camping. No one lives in the vicinity so it is fairly private and quiet at night. But during the day, and particularly on weekends, children of all ages come here to swim, play, and picnic.

BEACH HIKING/CAMPING

The hiking distance from the Río Lagartos Canal to Punta Holohit is 6 miles one way on sandy beach. Attractions are beachcombing and bird-watching.

When I get the city blues and want to get away from civilization, I head for the Río Lagartos Peninsula, where I know that unless I take along a mirror, I will not see a face for as long as I want. But I never feel alone there; nature is alive and well and I feel it all around me— thousands of water birds are everywhere, lizards crawl in the brush, and horseshoe crabs swim in the surf. Where in the city can one find such interesting company?

The 6-mile hike between the Río Lagartos Canal and Punta Holohit can be started at either point. It is a good idea to arrange for the boat that takes you to the peninsula to pick you up at the end of your trip.

If you don't make arrangements to be picked up, your best bet to get back to the mainland is to go to the Río Lagartos Canal. A few tourists are brought to the beach there almost every day. Fishing boats also go through the narrow canal, and for a small fee one will take you back to Río Lagartos.

Walk east from the canal toward Punta Holohit. The beach is narrow for the first mile, about 10 yards from the waterline to vegetation. At high tide the water meets the vegetation line in the narrowest beach stretches and you may have to wade in thigh-high water to continue the hike. The vegetation here consists of low brush and crawling cacti. These cacti are very abundant at this end of the peninsula up to about the third mile of the hike, when they gradually disappear. You should definitely wear hiking boots or some appropriate footwear if you go into the brush.

From the second to the fourth mile, the beach becomes much wider, reaching a width of about 150 yards. (Incidentally, the few tourists brought to the beach at the canal seldom venture past the first mile.) Here you will find an increasing array of shells, shell egg cases, coral pieces, driftwood, and other beachcombers' delights. In some places every square inch of sand is covered with shells as far as you can see. I call this area Playa Conchas (Shell Beach).

At about the fourth mile of the hike, the water and the vegetation lines meet again. Some 300 yards before you reach this point, you will spot a small group of fairly high bushes, the only cover found so far from the strong sun. This fact and the support the bushes provide for your tent make this area a very suitable place for camping. The beach is some 100 yards wide here and in normal weather there is no danger of the high tide coming more than 90 yards from the vegetation line.

On Playa Conchas, along with natural objects from the sea, you will find a number of man-made rejects that can be of use to you in your camp. On one of my camping trips here I found three empty wooden vegetable crates, which I used as table and seats, a one-gallon glass jug in which I carried water to extinguish the campfire, and an ample supply of firewood. This furniture and several utensils should still be hiding behind the bushes. On the same trip, since I arrived after a mild storm, I was lucky enough to find my dinner—two live edible conches washed ashore and three fish trapped in a small pond formed by the waves.

Continuing east from the campsite, you will find fewer and fewer shells until you reach a very wide area in which there are almost none. Now you can focus your attention on the many species of water birds that inhabit this part of the peninsula. This bird area is located between miles 4 and 5 and can be easily recognized, as the vegetation line recedes sharply, giving way to a large marsh covering several square acres, which is connected to one of the three shallow lagoons spreading from here to Punta Holohit.

If you are interested in birds, you would do well to have a water-bird field guide with you to help you identify them. Even without it, you might be able to recognize some of the families of sandpipers, plovers, and herons found here. With a little luck, you might see a group of pink flamingos from the sanctuary south of here.

This is one of my favorite spots on the peninsula. I can spend hours here watching birds with my binoculars or wading in the nearby lagoons, poking the shallow bottom with a long stick to find clams for dinner.

From the end of the marsh, it's only about a mile to Punta Holohit, the end of the peninsula. For the rest of the way the beach is about 10 yards wide. As you walk this last stretch you will find large numbers of horseshoe crabs or their empty shells measuring about 10 inches in length. Despite their name, these awkward creatures are closer relatives of spiders than of crabs and are absolutely harmless, but you should be careful not to step on their hard pointed tails. If you were thinking of a free lunch, forget it. There is as much meat in a horseshoe crab's leg as there is in the leg of a tarantula.

The area around the point is good for camping. There are large, clear sandy spots and plenty of high trees to provide shade. The only drawback to this spot as a campsite might be lack of privacy, due to the small groups of weekend tourists who come here across the estuary from San Felipe. If you choose your campsite well, you will have a good view of the sea, the estuary, and Isla de los Pájaros, west of the point. The Goddess of the Breezes keeps mosquitoes safely away most of the year.

If you want to catch a boat from here back to the mainland, the best days to try are Saturday and Sunday around noon.

SNORKELING

Unfortunately, in this part of the Yucatán Peninsula the water is seldom clear and in general it is not worth the trouble of packing your snorkeling gear.

SHORE FISHING

The shallow water and the numerous sandbars along the beach make fishing a bit tricky. Unless you are certain that you are casting in a deep, open area, your best bet would be to wade in the shallow water to a sandbar and fish in the open water beyond. For bait use the insides of horseshoe crabs, clams, or anything else suitable from the beach. Apart from the beach itself, other fishing spots are Punta Holohit on the estuary side and the Río Lagartos Canal.

QUINTANA ROO STATE

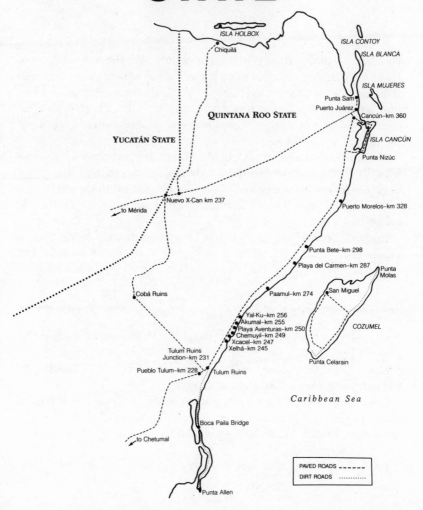

ISLA HOLBOX

Chiquilá

ISLA CONTOY

ISLA BLANCA

ISLA MUJERES

Punta Sam
Puerto Juárez

Cancún–km 360

QUINTANA ROO STATE

ISLA CANCÚN

YUCATÁN STATE

Punta Nizúc

Nuevo X-Can km 237

to Mérida

Puerto Morelos–km 328

Punta Bete–km 298

Playa del Carmen–km 287

Punta Molas

Cobá Ruins

Paamul–km 274

San Miguel

Yal-Ku–km 256
Akumal–km 255
Playa Aventuras–km 250
Chemuyil–km 249
Xcacel–km 247
Xelhá–km 245

COZUMEL

Tulum Ruins
Junction–km 231

Pueblo Tulum–km 228

Tulum Ruins

Punta Celarain

Caribbean Sea

Boca Paila Bridge

to Chetumal

PAVED ROADS ------
DIRT ROADS ....

Punta Allen

Isla Holbox

Paradise is many things to many people. To the inhabitants of Holbox, paradise would be a place with supermarkets, paved streets, TV reception, movie houses, and other conveniences of city life. Ironically, to young foreign travelers, Holbox is paradise because it doesn't have these conveniences, plus of course because of its natural attractions.

Isla Holbox is 15 miles long by 2 miles at its maximum width. The island's flat, swampy terrain is covered by brush and mangrove vegetation. The tiny town of Holbox is located on the western end of the island. Small-scale fishing is the main activity of its 700 inhabitants.

Holbox is not a lure to most tourists. Even though it has its own charm, sun, sand, and brine, it lacks hotels, restaurants, and other basic facilities.

Getting There

The passenger and car ferry terminal for Holbox is located in the tiny village of Chiquilá.

Bus   There are four daily direct buses from Valladolid to Chiquilá and they make ferry connections.

Car   The junction for Chiquilá is at km 237 of the Mérida–Puerto Juárez Highway. From here it is 75 km (46 miles) to Chiquilá over a good paved road. There is no gas station at Chiquilá, but there is one at Holbox.

Ferry Schedules   The tiny car ferry holds either two small cars, one large car, or one truck. The rates are cars 150 pesos, pickups 300 pesos. The ferry always makes the first run, but doesn't always make the second.

If you prefer to leave your car in Chiquilá while you visit Holbox, Don Chimay will keep a good eye on it. He lives right next to the pier and charges 20 pesos.

There are no places to stay in Chiquilá. There is a tiny refreshment stand, and two ladies, Doña Isidra and Doña Olga, serve plates of fried fish, beans, and rice to passersby.

Chiquilá to Holbox Island

Car Ferry	Passenger Ferry
8:00 A.M.	8:00 A.M.
4:30 P.M.	2:00 P.M.

Holbox Island to Chiquilá

Car Ferry	Passenger Ferry
5:00 A.M.	4:00 A.M.
2:00 P.M.	1:00 P.M.

Where to Stay

Apart from camping, rental houses are the other option for places to stay. Most of the houses consist of one or two rooms, have wood walls, cement floors, and *palapa* roofs. Some have running water, rest rooms, and showers. The furniture varies from nothing to a bed, a table, a couple of chairs, and a small gas stove. The price depends on the condition and furnishings of a particular house. A house with a bathroom and basic furniture rents for approximately 100 pesos a day.

From December through March, houses are in high demand, but it is not difficult to find sleeping space with one of the young visitors already renting a house.

The following people have houses for rent in Holbox: Don Avilio, Don Chelino, Don Domingo, Don Guach, Don Ines, Don Maximino, Don Pipo, and Doña Tomasa. (Don [masculine] and Doña [feminine] are Spanish titles used to indicate respect for a person's age, or social or economic position. The closest English equivalents are "Mr." and "Mrs.")

Restaurants

The only restaurant in Holbox is located half a block from the north side of the main plaza. It serves fried fish and other dishes depending on availability of beef, pork, etc.

Low-budget travelers can eat at Doña Zobeida's (2 blocks from the main plaza). Fried fish 50 pesos, beans 20 pesos, and all the tortillas you can eat.

The Beach

Isla Holbox's deserted beach is only 2 blocks from the main square. Although it faces the open sea, the water is very calm and the waves are only a few inches high. In places, you can walk a couple hundred yards into the sea with the water only coming up to knee height.

You can hike on the beach for a mile to the west end of the island and for over 2 miles east, up to where the vegetation merges with the sea. When you walk on the beach, wear sandals, and if you prefer to walk barefoot, keep an eye out for sharp, broken shells.

There is no other beach on the Yucatán Peninsula where a beachcomber can find more species or greater quantities of shells. In fact, there are so many shells here that more than one beachcomber (including myself) has been tempted to go into the wholesale shell business. But beachcombing is not amassing or exploiting the gifts and surprises of the sea. Beachcombing is walking, relaxing, and hunting for memories and discoveries in the shape of shells and other treasures of the sea. Among the shells you will find here are lightning whelks, rude pen shells, turkey wings, cup-and-saucer shells, lion's paws, in-curved cap shells, common dove shells, common Atlantic bubbles, and giant Atlantic cockles.

A to Z

BAKERY (Panadería)

East side of the main plaza. The bread is good and cheap (10 pesos for foot-long loaf) but you'll have to go through a lot of pushing and shoving before you can get your hands on an oven-hot loaf. Be there before 8:00 A.M.

BANKS

The closest bank is in Kantunilkín 44 km (27 miles) south of Chiquilá.

GROCERY STORES

There are three grocery stores on the east side of the main plaza.

POST OFFICE

At Kantunilkín.

TELEGRAPH OFFICE

Located 2 blocks from the main plaza toward the ferry pier.

TELEPHONE OFFICE

At Kantunilkín.

PUERTO JUÁREZ

The passenger ferry terminal for Isla Mujeres is located in Puerto Juárez. Before Cancún was invented, Puerto Juárez was the only town of any size on the mainland across from Isla Mujeres. Now, the neighbor is moving in and it is more accurate to say that tiny Puerto Juárez is a suburb of Cancún.

Getting There

Bus   There are several direct bus runs between Mérida–Puerto Juárez, Tulum–Puerto Juárez, and vice versa. The bus station here is 50 yards from the ferry terminal. City buses service Cancún and Puerto Juárez every 30 minutes. You are allowed to carry your luggage on the bus.

Passenger Ferry Schedule   The fare is 25 pesos. Day visitors to Isla Mujeres may leave their cars at the free parking lot by the pier.

To Isla Mujeres	To Puerto Juárez
5:30 A.M.	6:45 A.M.
9:00 A.M.	9:45 A.M.
10:30 A.M.	11:45 A.M.
12:30 P.M.	1:45 P.M.
2:30 P.M.	3:45 P.M.
3:30 P.M.	5:45 P.M.
6:30 P.M.	
7:15 P.M.	

Where to Stay

There are a few hotels near the pier in Puerto Juárez in case you miss the last ferry to Isla Mujeres.

BUDGET

Hotel Los Faroles   Double, 700 pesos. Hot water and ceiling fans.

Hotel Janet   Double, 900 pesos. Hot water, ceiling fans.

MODERATE

Hotel Isabel   Double, 1,000 pesos. Air conditioning, hot water, pool, restaurant, long-distance office.

PUNTA SAM

The car ferry terminal for Isla Mujeres is located at Punta Sam, 5 kilometers north of Puerto Juárez.

Getting There

Bus   City buses from Cancún supposedly run to make connection with the car ferry here. The bus often arrives when the ferry has already gone, or leaves before the ferry arrives.

Vehicle Ferry   Leaves Monday through Sunday. The fare is 55 pesos for cars, and 6 pesos for passengers.

Get your car in line at least 15 minutes before departure. There are separate lines for trucks and cars. The ferry holds about 16 cars. If there are that many cars and trucks ahead of your vehicle, you will have to wait 3 hours until the next ferry.

To Isla Mujeres	To Punta Sam
7:15 A.M.	6:30 A.M.
10:00 A.M.	11:00 A.M.
1:15 P.M.	2:00 P.M.
4:00 P.M.	5:00 P.M.

Where to Stay

There are no hotels in Punta Sam.

Camping Almirante de Gante *Km 4, Puerto Juárez–Punta Sam Highway.* There are "shady" campgrounds that promise you the sun and give it to you with all its blistering hot rays. These campgrounds may also offer an ample supply of water and hot "showers," but . . . you have to wait until the rainy season.

There are also shady campgrounds that do not promise anything and give you a coconut grove, hot showers 24 hours a day, and enough water to start your own rainy season. Camping de Gante is this kind of campground and it also offers a sunny beach, clean grounds, a picnic *palapa*, children's games, and an inexpensive restaurant with good seafood. Camping rates are 50 pesos per person, Rent-a-tent 100 pesos, and double trailer space is 100 pesos per vehicle.

Isla Mujeres

Paradise comes in all sizes, and Isla Mujeres is a little paradise of white, sandy beaches and warm turquoise water. What to do in paradise is a matter of individual choice and the choices in Isla Mujeres range from tanning on the beach, drinking *coco locos,* and counting sand grains (optional) to snorkeling (a must), scuba diving, fishing, and boating.

Isla Mujeres ("Island of Women") acquired its name from the female icons found on the island at the time of its discovery by the Spanish conquerors in 1517. It's a small island 5 miles by ½ mile at its widest point, and 300 yards at its narrowest point (the 2 block-long Calle Allende).

Throughout the island the vegetation consists of low trees and brush, except for the northern end where the city is located. There, tall coconut trees abound, giving the island its piña colada flavor. The city is only 5 blocks wide and 10 blocks long and has approximately 3,000 inhabitants.

The main hotels, restaurants, and shops are to be found near Calle Hidalgo, the main street. At the end of this street is the city's main plaza, as is the city hall, the police station, the city's only church, the biggest supermarket, the movie house, and the basketball court. Other stores, restaurants, hotels, the ferry terminals, and long-distance phone stations can be found within a 3-block radius of the main plaza.

Getting There

Isla Mujeres is located 5 miles off the northeastern point of the Yucatán Peninsula. Ferries for Isla Mujeres leave from Puerto Juárez, 5 miles north of Cancún. Puerto Juárez is well connected by

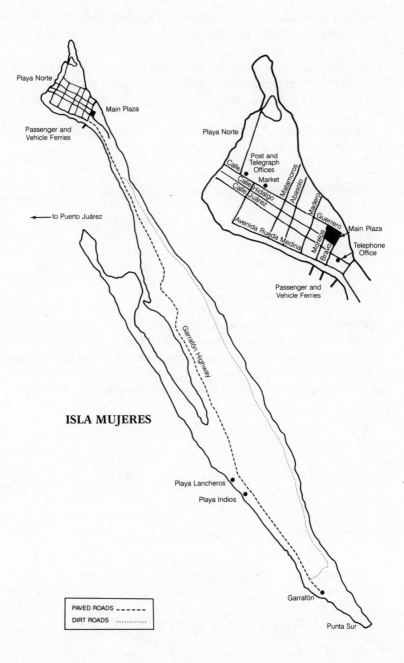

Playa Norte

Main Plaza

Passenger and
Vehicle Ferries

← to Puerto Juárez

Garrafón Highway

ISLA MUJERES

Playa Lancheros

Playa Indios

Garrafón

Punta Sur

Playa Norte

Post and
Telegraph
Offices

Market

Calle

Calle Hidalgo

Calle Juárez

Matamoros

Abasolo

Madero

Guerrero

Morelos

Bravo

Avenida Rueda Medina

Main Plaza

Telephone
Office

Passenger and
Vehicle Ferries

PAVED ROADS ------
DIRT ROADS ....

taxis and city buses from Cancún, and buses from Mérida and Chetumal arrive 24 hours a day. Cancún is the closest international airport for Isla Mujeres.

Car   Puerto Juárez is 320 km from Mérida at the end of Highway 180. (To take your vehicle into Isla Mujeres, see ferry schedule.) If you don't want to take your car to the island, you can park it next to the pier in Puerto Juárez.

Passenger Ferry   The fare is 25 pesos for the 30-minute ride to Isla. Buy your ticket on the ferry.

To Isla Mujeres	To Puerto Juárez
5:30 A.M.	6:45 A.M.
9:00 A.M.	9:45 A.M.
10:30 A.M.	11:45 A.M.
12:30 P.M.	1:45 P.M.
2:30 P.M.	3:45 P.M.
3:30 P.M.	5:45 P.M.
6:30 P.M.	
7:15 P.M.	

Vehicle Ferries   Punta Sam, 3 miles north of Puerto Juárez, is the port of access for Isla Mujeres for vehicles and their passengers.

The fare for cars is 55 pesos, passengers 6 pesos. Line up and buy tickets 30 minutes before departure. Riding time is 30 minutes. (For additional information on ferries, see the Puerto Juárez and Punta Sam sections of this book.)

To Isla Mujeres	To Punta Sam
7:15 A.M.	6:30 A.M.
10:00 A.M.	11:00 A.M.
1:15 P.M.	2:00 P.M.
4:00 P.M.	5:00 P.M.

Where to Stay

Accommodations in Isla Mujeres consist mostly of budget hotels in the 500-peso range. There are also four medium-priced hotels, two deluxe hotels, and a hostel. On the southern end of the island there is a campground.

Some of the budget hotels are family run and have conventlike rules: no visitors of the opposite sex in the rooms, no late returns, and other rules that don't mix with free-spirited vacationers.

─────────────────── **BUDGET** ───────────────────

Poc Na Hostel   Poc Na is the only place in Isla Mujeres for travelers on tight budgets. At present there are 68 sturdy wooden bunk beds, distributed in six sections, each with a shower, toilet, and washbasins. The hammock section burned down in December 1981 during the island's festivities, when a firecracker fell on the hostel's *palapa* roof.

The 200-peso fee pays for a bunk bed and a large backpack-size locker. A 100-peso key deposit is charged when checking in. Towels, sheets, padded mats, and blankets are available for rent. Pay your rent before 1:00 P.M. to avoid paying a 7-peso penalty.

Poc Na's large dining area serves as its social center. There, under the same *palapa* roof, young people from all over the world gather to exchange travel information, experiences, and tastes of papaya, mamey, mango, and other newfound foods.

Just about every conversation in this mini-delegation of the United Nations seems to start with: "Is anyone sitting here?," "Where are you from?" and "Where did you buy your _____?" (fill in the blank with hammock, bread, peanut butter, etc.). Any line and bait is good when you are fishing for friends here. As people talk, play table games, read, or write piles of postcards, the background music is provided by Poc Na's electronic jukebox, with such appropriate selections as "Back to the Island," "Here Comes the Sun," "Yucatán Café," and "This Is My Year for Mexico."

Poc Na is indeed a pleasant place to stay, but it has some disadvantages. It's noisy. The only quiet hours are between midnight and 6:00 A.M. It doesn't have a safe place to keep valuables. The sturdy lockers have on several occasions been broken into and robbed of cameras, money, and passports.

Hotel Isla Mujeres   *Calle Hidalgo at southeast corner of main plaza.* Double, 500 pesos. Ceiling fans, cold water. Basic and clean.

Hotel María de los Angeles   *Juárez 24.* Double, 500 pesos. Ceiling fans, hot water, motellike. All rooms have independent entrance.

Hotel Xul-Ha *Calle Hidalgo, 4 blocks north of plaza.* Double, 500 pesos. Ceiling fans, hot water. Pleasant family run hotel.

Hotel Margarita *Malecón 9.* Double, 500 pesos. Ceiling fans, cold water. Has only 8 rooms. Clean.

Hotel Osorio *Madero 10.* Double, 600 pesos. Ceiling fans, hot water. Clean and pleasant.

Hotel María José *Madero and Malecón.* Double, 600 pesos. Ceiling fans, hot water. Nice for the price.

Hotel Martinez *Madero.* Double, 600 pesos. Ceiling fans, hot water. Strict, family run hotel. Sometimes unfriendly. The owners may, for example, refuse to show you a room.

Hotel Marcianito *Abasolo 10.* Double, 700 pesos. Ceiling fans. Hot water. Clean. Strict, family run.

Hotel el Paso *In front of passenger ferry.* Double, 700 pesos. Ceiling fans, hot water.

Hotel Caracol *Matamoros 5.* Double, 700 pesos. Ceiling fans, hot water. Cooking facilities included in price.

Hotel Las Palmas *Guerrero 20.* Double, 700 pesos. Ceiling fans, hot water. Has a little patio.

Autel Carmelina *Madero and Guerrero.* Double, 700 pesos. Ceiling fans, hot water. Large, clean rooms. Has parking space in front of rooms.

Hotel San Luis *Madero and Guerrero.* Double, 700 pesos. Ceiling fans, hot water. Motellike. Has only 4 rooms.

——————————————— MODERATE ———————————————

(Add 5 percent tax to room rates)

Hotel Caribe Maya *Madero 9.* Double, 900 pesos. Ceiling fans, hot water. Modern.

Hotel Berny *Juárez and Abasolo.* Double, 1,400 pesos. Ceiling fans, hot water, phone in room, small pool, laundry service. Tel. 20025.

Cabañas *Playa Norte.* Double, 1,100 pesos. Ceiling fans, hot water. Right on the beach in shady coconut grove. Very attractive.

Hotel Rocamar *Bravo and Guerrero.* Double, 1,600 pesos. Ceiling fans or air conditioning, hot water, restaurant, bar, parking lot. Very clean, great sea view, and genuinely friendly. Tel. 20101.

─────────────── **DELUXE** ───────────────

Hotel Posada del Mar *Malecón.* Double, 3,500 pesos with breakfast and dinner. Rooms with meals only. Air conditioning, pool, gardens, restaurant, bar, view. In front of the beach. The best and most pleasant hotel in town. Tel. 20195.

━━━━━━━━━ *Restaurants* ━━━━━━━━━

When it comes to food, variety is not the spice of life and spice is not the life of food in the restaurants of Isla Mujeres. The menus of Isla's restaurants look like mimeographed sheets. They all serve pretty much the same food—soup, seafoods, beef, poultry, breakfasts. Only the prices and the food stains on the menus are different. One hopes the day will come when Isla will have a pizzeria, a taquería (taco stand), and other diverse foods that will give a little more flavor to its life.

The dinner prices quoted below are for a medium-priced meal consisting of soup, fish plate, and a beer or glass of wine.

Restaurant La Mano de Dios *Calle Hidalgo.* A popular restaurant with the budget crowd. Although it is good and inexpensive, the portions are commensurate with the prices. When they are very busy, the portions seem to get even smaller. It has some outdoor tables. No beer or wine. Dinner approximately 200 pesos.

Restaurant Giltry *Calle Hidalgo.* At this budget restaurant the food is good, the portions are reasonable, but the atmosphere is sterile. It has some cool outdoor tables. Sells beer. Dinner approximately 230 pesos.

Restaurant Estrellita Marinera *Calle Hidalgo.* A small, uncrowded family run restaurant with some outdoor tables. It has a limited menu and offers lunch specials. No beer. Dinner 210 pesos.

Restaurant Tropicana *In front of car ferry.* Popular with the locals. Has an ample menu. Sells beer. Dinner approximately 250 pesos.

Restaurant Dhaymaru *Juárez.* Has an ample menu and offers good food and service. The patio tables at the back are private and quiet. Dinner approximately 300 pesos.

Restaurant Brisas del Caribe *One block north of the passenger ferry, on the Malecón.* Has a limited menu of lunch and dinner specials. Open air, right by the waterfront, a good place to watch sunsets and enjoy the night breeze. Dinner approximately 300 pesos.

Restaurant Gomar *Hidalgo.* One of the cleaner, better restaurants on the island. Offers an ample menu, well-prepared food, wine list, good service, and some atmosphere. Has some outdoor tables. Dinner approximately 350 pesos plus tax.

Ciro's Lobster House *Guerrero and Matamoros.* Ciro's is the town's fancy restaurant. It's air-conditioned, has a full bar, an ample menu and wine list, and good service. Dinner approximately 400 pesos plus tax.

Kan Kin María's French Restaurant *Km 5.5, road to Garrafón.* The biggest, ugliest concrete sign you have ever seen marks the entrance to Kan Kin on the Garrafón Highway, but good food is served here. *Belle meunière* fish fillet, rabbit provençal, and other French delicacies are among the house specialties. The food is as much a delight to the palate as the view is to the eye. María's has its own pier, so you can drop by for lunch from New Orleans, Miami, and even Cancún. Open daily noon to 6:00 P.M.

─────────────── **FOOD STANDS** ───────────────

No Name Hamburger Stand *Main Plaza.* Serves hamburgers, tortas, shish kebab, desserts, and juices. Open 6:00 P.M. to 11:00 P.M.

No Name II *Main Plaza (under the city's water tower).* Besides chicken consommé, *salbutes,* and tostadas, this little stand serves the best and most filling Yucatán-style chicken tamales on the island, at 30 pesos apiece.

Supertortas and Tacos Andale *Hidalgo.* Chicken, pork roast *(pierna)*, and *chorizo* tortas are the specialty here. The tortas are only 30 pesos apiece and they are prepared by Miss Smiles herself (you'll recognize her right away). Open 6:00 P.M. to 11:00 P.M.

Nightlife

If you are looking for a wild bar and disco scene, you won't find it in sleepy Isla Mujeres, where local families spend their evenings at home. That's not to say, though, that it doesn't have its own peculiar version of a nightlife, created by the floating tourist crowd. Gathered together in a local restaurant, tourists come in as many different species as the inhabitants of the nearby bird sanctuaries— and with as many different chirps. The Mexican tourists speak Spanish and a little English, and the Texans speak a little English along with their Texan. Assorted Americans and Canadians add their own specialized versions of English, and the Europeans seem to speak a bit of everything. Despite such adverse linguistic circumstances, after two or three margaritas, the determination to communicate overcomes the limitations. All at once interpreters, lip-readers, and sign-language acrobats abound, and before you know it, everyone is speaking languages they didn't know they spoke, meeting friends they didn't know they had, exchanging toasts, and buying each other drinks. Invariably at the end of the evening a frantic exchange of addresses ensues and final farewells are made: "orevuar," "good baee," "adeeos," etc.

Outside of the restaurant scene, the real nightlife in Isla Mujeres happens in the main square and in the first 4 tiny blocks of Calle Hidalgo, which are closed to traffic. This is the favorite strolling area of the local population and tourists. Entire families go there to walk, eat in a restaurant, or watch their children play in the plaza playground of concrete animal sculptures, swings, and slides. There is also the local movie house, where for a few pesos you can see American and European movies with Spanish subtitles. Occasionally civic and cultural events are held in the plaza. There is a basketball court there and games are held almost every night. Quite often impromptu games are held between the local teams and those of tourists.

ROMANTIC SPOTS

Many places that are busy and noisy under the sun's rays are transformed into quiet, romantic spots under the light of the moon, with tropic warmth and the sound of the surf. The tiny beach at the north end of Calle Matamoros, Garrafón, and Playa Norte are a few of my favorite romantic spots on Isla Mujeres.

Beaches and Activities

Playa Norte, located on the northern edge of town, is the island's best and most accessible beach and is within easy walking distance from any part of town. You can wade far into the calm turquoise sea, 100 yards or more, and still the water only comes to waist level. Because the beach is on the protected, leeward side of the island, there is rarely a ripple to disturb the water surface.

As is the case throughout the Yucatán Peninsula, the sand here is white and fine and it's a sweet pleasure to lie on it to catch the sun, take a siesta, or read a book. At the west end of the beach there are two restaurants with thatched roofs where you can buy a lunch of fried fish and soft drinks, beer, and mixed drinks.

There are three other beaches, listed below, south of the town along the highway on the west side of the island. It's a hot but scenic one-hour walk to Garrafón, the last beach at the end of the 6-kilometer road (described under Snorkeling). Taxi fare is 150 pesos one way to Garrafón. Make arrangements with the taxi driver to pick you up later.

You can rent a bicycle or a motorbike from one of the bike shops downtown. See A to Z section, "Bicycles and Motorcycles."

Playa Lancheros, Km 4, is a very safe, shallow beach and has a few shade trees. It is uncrowded until around noon, when the island's tour boats unload a few dozen people who come to watch the giant sea turtles that are kept in captivity here.

There is a large picnic *palapa* and soft drinks for sale here, but there is no food.

Playa Indios, Km 4.5, is more than a beach. This is the island's only campground. See "Camping."

El Garrafón, Km 6, is described in detail in the Snorkeling section.

SNORKELING

Garrafón is the island's best snorkeling area. Various species of brilliantly colored fish swim along the rocky shoreline, while a few yards offshore, schools of Bermuda chubs swim almost at the water surface among the snorkelers. A few feet deeper, schools of white, blue-striped, and French grunts paint the water many colors.

The topography of Garrafón's shoreline seems to have been designed by nature to accommodate both beginning and advanced snorkelers. Up to 20 yards from the shoreline the water is very shallow, 3 feet and less in depth, where a beginner can practice without fear of deep water or waves. Care must be taken, though, to avoid being scratched by rocks in some of the shallower spots.

Beyond this area, advanced snorkelers will find the water more suitable to their expertise. Here the depth drops abruptly from 3 to 18 feet. Although the water can be choppy, unless you swim about 100 yards out into the sea, there is no undertow or current. The best and safest access into the deep sea is a passage between the rocks, located toward the wooden pier on the right as you face the sea.

Garrafón is a very popular tourist spot and it can get crowded. To avoid the crowds, go early in the morning before 10:00 or late in the afternoon after 4:00 when it's almost empty.

Garrafón has a restaurant and bar with good seafood. Lunch costs approximately 350 pesos. A cheaper lunch alternative is MacMa-yan's Hamburgers by the main entrance gate. Burgers are 100 pesos, fish and fries 60.

Snorkeling equipment is available for rent at 70 pesos a set (snorkel, mask, and fins). Admission to Garrafón is 10 pesos.

Playa Norte The underwater visibility is only about 20 feet, but the entire beach is an ideal place to learn how to snorkel. Experienced snorkelers can try the east end of the beach by the wooden pier, where visibility is about 100 feet. When the sea is rough, don't snorkel beyond the rocks at this point.

The windward side of the island is also an excellent snorkeling area. A word of caution, however, the entire shoreline here is covered with sharp rocks. Care must be used when going in and out of the water. Even on a calm day, a small wave can push you against a sharp rock. When the sea is rough, snorkeling is very dangerous and should be avoided altogether.

SCUBA DIVING

Before Cancún existed, Cuevones, Chital, La Bandera, and Manchones reefs were Isla's own reefs. Now Isla Mujeres and Cancún share these reefs, and despite an increase in the number of divers here, there is a sea of room and scenery for all to share.

In diving circles Isla Mujeres is famous for its sleeping shark caves. However, more than a diving attraction, this has become a promotional lure. Dive shops will tell you there is a 50-50 chance you'll see a sleeping shark if you visit the caves. Personally I'm not willing to get close to a sleeping German shepherd, much less a sleeping tiger shark. Confine your dives to the safe reefs. For additional information, see "Scuba Diving" in the Cancún section.

Mexico Divers *Avenida Rueda Medina.* 50 aluminum and steel tanks, Mako 7.5 CFM compressor, 28-foot outboard motorboat, 875 pesos for 2 tanks and lunch, instruction costs 925 pesos for a 5-hour PADI resort course. Tel. 20131.

El Canon Dive Shop Tank refills only.

DEEP-SEA FISHING

Mexico Divers *Avenida Rueda Medina.* The 31-foot Berthram with 2 chairs and 4 lines is the only deep-sea fishing boat in Isla Mujeres. The full-day 7,500-peso charge includes bait, tackle, and snacks.

SHORE FISHING

There are two fair fishing spots within walking distance of town. At the wooden pier at Playa Norte, use any bait, spoons, or plugs for jacks and other fish, or fish for grunts and other pan-size fish at the boat harbor north of the ferry landing.

Punta Sur is at the southern end of the island. To get there, go first to Garrafón and then take the dirt road that continues down to the point by the lighthouse. The locals fish here with sturdy hand lines and medium-size hooks, but lighter tackle can be used. For bait you can use whole ballyhoo *(escribano)* which can be purchased at the Malecón, or any cut bait. Snappers, groupers, and jacks are common catch here.

CAMPING

There is no campground within easy walking distance of town. Camping is allowed in Playa Norte, the town's main beach, only in the peak of high season (Christmas) when every hotel in town is full to capacity. The only campground on the island is 5 km (3 miles) from the center of town.

Indios Campground, Km 4.5, Garrafón Road, is on a nice stretch of beach, has a fairly shady coconut grove, but is dumpy and has filthy bathrooms. No electricity. Camping rate: 60 pesos per person.

Tours

The Cooperativa de Pescadores runs three daily boat tours to Playa Lancheros and Garrafón. The tours are made in canopied outboard motorboats with capacity for approximately 14 passengers and last a total of 4 hours. The 500-peso fare includes a lunch of grilled fish and shrimp or conch ceviche. Departures are from the passenger ferry pier at 10:00 A.M., 12 noon, and 1:30 P.M. Reserve beforehand.

CONTOY EXCURSION

Contoy Island is a bird sanctuary located about 18 miles north of Isla Mujeres. The island is about 4 miles long by ¼ mile wide and its only inhabitants are birds and a couple of employees of the biological station there. Contoy is the home of thousands of olivaceous cormorants, brown pelicans, and "magnificent frigate" birds. Great white herons, reddish egrets (white and dark phases), and about a dozen other bird species are found in lesser numbers.

Ricardo Gaitan conducts a 2-day Contoy excursion in his 30-foot *Providencia* sailboat. The trip is a combination of sailing, fishing, snorkeling, bird-watching, and camping. On a typical Contoy excursion the *Providencia* sets sail from Isla Mujeres at 10:00 A.M. on the first day. As you sail toward Contoy you will be trolling for barracuda under the supervision of Ricardo. Halfway between Isla Mujeres and Contoy, the *Providencia* will anchor for an hour or so of snorkeling.

When you arrive at Contoy, Ricardo will prepare a lunch of charcoal-grilled barracuda. The rest of the day is spent hiking, swimming, snorkeling, and doing whatever you please, and that night you'll sleep on the beach.

On the morning of the second day, you'll sail to some prime bird-watching spots. While you watch brown pelicans dive into the water for their breakfast, you'll eat one of Ricardo's delicious omelets. Around noon you'll return to the beach for lunch. By 5:00 P.M. you'll be back at Isla Mujeres.

The cost of the excursion is 800 pesos per person and includes meals, refreshments, and snorkeling equipment. Remember to take along sunscreen or suntan lotion, mosquito repellent, and a sleeping bag or a blanket. For reservations, see Ricardo at the Cooperativa, Isla Mujeres, or at Poc Na Hostel, where he usually hangs out.

It's a Steal

One way to find out if a dog will eat meat is to leave unguarded a ham leg, a few steaks, and, why not, a few hot dogs too. Likewise, one way to find out if thieves will steal is to leave unguarded your camera, money, and other valuables where a well-trained retriever can make them change owner in a fraction of a second.

Basically, the Yucatán Peninsula is a very safe place from thieves and pickpockets. But it's better to prevent than to regret.

1. Traveler's checks are a fantastic invention. Use them. Keep sales receipts and numbers separate. They are essential for refunds.

2. In crowds and crowded buses (Mérida and Cancún), do not carry your wallet in your back pocket.

3. On busy beaches, always keep your possessions within sight when you go for a swim or buy a drink, etc. Keep cameras and other valuables out of sight so you won't target yourself as someone worth robbing.

A to Z

BAKERY

Panadería La Reina *Madero and Juárez.* Open from 7:00 A.M. to 10:00 A.M. and 3:00 P.M. to 8:00 P.M. Good sweet rolls *(pan dulce)* and French bread *(pan blanco)*.

BANKS

Banco del Atlantico *Juárez 5.* Money exchange hours are from 10:30 A.M. to 12 noon only.

Banpais *Juárez 3.* Money exchange hours are 9:30 A.M. to 1:30 P.M.

BICYCLES

Hotel María Isabel *Madero and Malecón.* Bicycles rent for 20 pesos an hour.

CURVES

On the road to Garrafón, watch out for the very sharp unmarked curves between km 3 and 4. Drive at a speed no greater than 20 mph through this area.

FISH

If you have cooking facilities, you can buy fresh fish for 180 pesos a kilo a block and a half south of the car ferry.

HEALTH CENTER

Centro de Salud *Calle Guerrero at the main plaza.* It is open from 8:00 A.M. to 8:00 P.M. Emergency services are provided 24 hours a day. The fee is 100 pesos for non-Mexicans.

MARKET

Guerrero and Matamoros Isla's tiny market offers a better selection of fruits and vegetables than the supermarkets, but that's about all. There is a fried-fish stand at the entrance where you can buy pan-sized fried fish for 200 pesos a kilo.

MOTORCYCLES

You can rent small 70cc motorbikes for touring the island. Rates are standard in all motorbike rental shops *(rentadoras).* Rates: 2 hours (minimum) 120 pesos, 5 hours for 500 pesos, 10 hours for 1,000 pesos. Deposit of 500 pesos. Rental shops: Cicero Rodriguez, Madero 19; Gomar on Hidalgo; Rentadora Joaquin, Juárez 7.

POST OFFICE

The post office is located at Guerrero 15, open 8:00 A.M. to 1:00 P.M. and 3:00 to 6:00 P.M. on weekdays, and from 9:00 A.M. to 12 noon on Saturday. You can receive mail through general delivery. Mail is held for 10 days and is then returned to sender. Have your letters addressed to: Your Name, Lista de Correos, Isla Mujeres, Quintana Roo, Mexico.

SUPERMARKETS

Isla Mujeres has two well-stocked supermarkets where you can find meat, vegetables, fruit, canned goods, liquor, and toiletries. Hard liquor and beer are not sold on Sunday, but wine is.

Super Betino, Main Plaza, is larger and better stocked and open 7:00 A.M. to 9:00 P.M.

Super Mirtita, Juárez and Bravo, open 6:00 A.M. to 12 noon and 4:00 P.M. to 8:00 P.M.

TAXI FARES

From downtown Isla Mujeres to:

	Pesos
Playa Lancheros	120
Playa Indios	130
Kan Kin María's Restaurant	150
Garrafón	150

These rates are for a maximum of 5 passengers.

TELEGRAPH OFFICE

Located next to the post office at Guerrero 13.

Open 9:00 A.M. to 8:30 P.M. daily and 9:00 A.M. to noon holidays, Saturday, and Sunday. Telegrams and money orders should be addressed to: Your Name, Lista de Telégrafos, Isla Mujeres, Quintana Roo, Mexico. They are held for 10 days and then returned to sender.

The *larga distancia* office (long distance) is located at Juárez and Bravo. Open 8:00 A.M. to 12 noon and 3:00 to 8:00 P.M. There is a 100-peso service charge for collect calls not accepted and a 30-peso service charge for accepted collect calls.

Cancún

In 1967 the Mexican government sponsored a computer study to choose the site of a new beach resort on Mexico's east coast. Because of its location, spectacular beaches, and room for growth, Cancún was chosen, and it has now grown from a village of 100 fishermen to a city of 60,000 people. Baby Cancún may well be the only beach resort born from Mother Nature and Father Computer. By the year 2000, Cancún is programmed to grow from its present hotel capacity of 6,000 rooms to 20,000 rooms. Cancún is divided into two main areas: Cancún City and Cancún Island.

Most of the stores, banks, government offices, post and telegraph offices, Cancún's two markets, budget hotels, and restaurants are located in Cancún City.

Cancún City's downtown area is located on Avenida Tulum between Avenida Uxmal to the north and Avenida Cobá to the south. Here in the cool shade of tropical trees, you'll find pleasant sidewalk restaurants, beachwear and import shops, banks, grocery stores, and some of the city's budget hotels.

Don't overlook Avenida Tulum's cross streets (Claveles, Tulipanes, etc.), where you'll find eating places that range from taco stands to fancy international restaurants. Four tiny blocks west and parallel to Avenida Tulum is Avenida Yaxchilán, where you'll find quite a few budget hotels and restaurants.

Cancún Island is only a stone's throw from the mainland and is connected to it by two bridges. All of Cancún's beaches and its fanciest hotels are found on this long, narrow strip of sand, also known as the hotel zone.

In and around the Convention Center on Cancún Island are several shopping malls and plazas. Restaurants and airline and car rental offices are also found in this area.

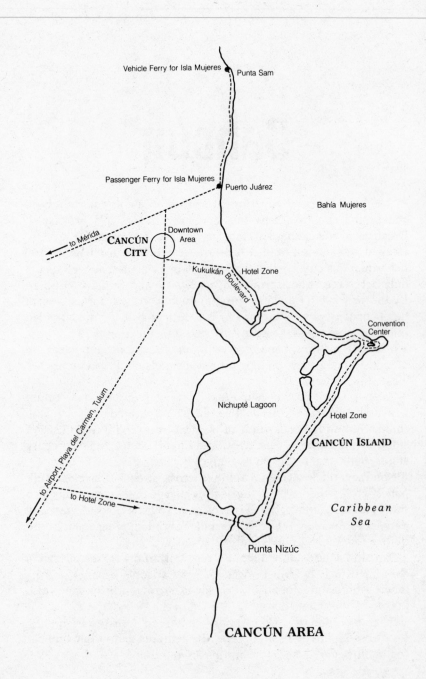

Vehicle Ferry for Isla Mujeres ● Punta Sam

Passenger Ferry for Isla Mujeres ■ Puerto Juárez

Bahía Mujeres

to Mérida

CANCÚN CITY

Downtown Area

Kukulkán Boulevard

Hotel Zone

Convention Center

to Airport, Playa del Carmen, Tulum

Nichupté Lagoon

Hotel Zone

CANCÚN ISLAND

to Hotel Zone →

Caribbean Sea

Punta Nizúc

CANCÚN AREA

Kukulkán Boulevard (also called Cancún Boulevard) runs the length of the island and connects all the hotels and beaches there with downtown Cancún. City buses stop at designated stops on Kukulkán, and taxis cruise the boulevard or park at hotel entrances.

Getting There

By Airplane Aeromexico, Mexicana, Continental, Eastern, Lacsa, and United Airlines have regular schedules into Cancún. From the United States there are direct flights from Houston, Dallas, New Orleans, Miami, New York, and Chicago. The Cancún airport is 20 km south of Cancún City. (See "Airport" in the A to Z section.) Aerocaribe and Aerocozumel have numerous daily flights from Cozumel to Cancún. Flying time is 15 minutes and the round-trip fare is 850 pesos plus tax.

Bus Buses leave Mérida for Cancún about every 2 hours. The trip takes 4 hours on ADO first-class buses.

Car Cancún is 320 km (199 miles) east of Mérida on Highway 180.

Getting Around Cancún

It's easy to get around on foot in downtown Cancún. The downtown area is only 5 blocks long and 2 blocks wide. Cancún's tiny blocks are about half the size of an American city block.

Buses City buses abound and connect downtown Cancún with the hotel zone and with neighboring towns. They run from 6:00 A.M. to 10:00 P.M. There are two bus routes most frequently used by visitors to Cancún. The Ruta 1–Zona Hotelera runs from downtown Cancún to the hotel zone as far as the Sheraton Hotel. Catch it going south at *parada* (bus stop) signs on Avenida Tulum downtown and along Kukulkán Boulevard in the hotel zone. The fare is 5 pesos. The Ruta 1–Cancún–Puerto Juárez–Punta Sam buses to Puerto Juárez (the passenger ferry terminal for Isla Mujeres) run about every 30 minutes and less frequently after 7:00 P.M. Catch them going north on Tulum. The fare is 5 pesos.

Buses to Punta Sam are supposed to allow you to connect with the car ferry there, but too often the bus arrives when the ferry has already gone or leaves before the ferry arrives. The fare is 10 pesos.

Taxis Taxis cruise the main avenues until about 11:00 P.M. Fares quoted below are for up to 5 passengers (without luggage) and for one destination without stops. Expect higher rates when, for example, there is a group of three people and one is going to the Verano Beat Hotel, another to the Calinda, and the last one to El Presidente Hotel. All these hotels are in the same rate zone (100 pesos) but many drivers will count this as three different rides (300 pesos). To avoid arguments with drivers, ask for the rate to your destination before getting in.

Taxi fares
From downtown Cancún to:

Camino Real Hotel and points before it	100 pesos
Sheraton Hotel and points before it	110 pesos
Airport	300 pesos
Puerto Juárez	100 pesos

Rides within the downtown area are 60 pesos.
From the hotel zone to the airport: 200 pesos.

To tour the ruins and other nearby attractions, a taxi can be hired at a reasonable rate per person, depending on the destination, number of passengers, and whether the taxi is a small European or large American model. These rates include a waiting period.

Long-distance taxi rates
From the hotel zone:

to Tulum	2,200 pesos
to Xelha	2,400 pesos
to Chichén Itzá	2,800 pesos
to Cobá	2,500 pesos

Where to Stay

There are two hotel areas in Cancún: the downtown zone, consisting mostly of moderately priced hotels, with double rooms in the 1,000- to 2,000-peso range, and the beach hotel zone, with fancy beachfront hotels, where a double room costs anywhere from 4,000 to 9,000 pesos.

BUDGET (Downtown)

Hotel El Arabe   *Avenidas Yaxchilán and Cobá.* Double, 600 pesos. Ceiling fans, hot water, 23 rooms.

CANCÚN

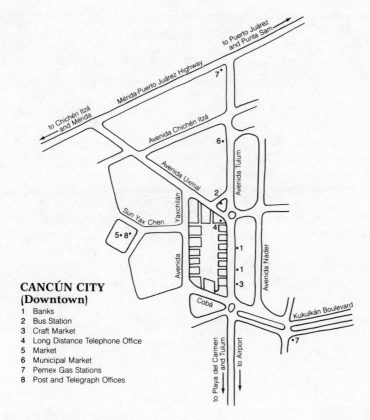

**CANCÚN CITY
(Downtown)**

1 Banks
2 Bus Station
3 Craft Market
4 Long Distance Telephone Office
5 Market
6 Municipal Market
7 Pemex Gas Stations
8 Post and Telegraph Offices

Hotel Colonial   *Tulipanes #22.* Double, 900 pesos. Ceiling fans, hot water. Clean.

Hotel Yaxché   *Avenida Cobá #41.* Double, 900 pesos. Air conditioning, hot water. Clean. 8 rooms only. Tel. 40090.

Hotel Plaza Tulum   *Avenida Tulum #13.* Double, 450 pesos plus tax. Air conditioning, hot water. 11 rooms. Clean.

──────────────── **MODERATE** ────────────────

All the hotels in this price range have air conditioning and hot water.

Hotel Coral   *Avenida Sun Yax Chen #51.* Double, 1,000 pesos. Small pool. Tel. 40586.

The Street System

Cancún's street system is like a group of interwoven spider webs, and although streets and avenues are generally well marked, it can be a little tricky to get around.

The principal avenues are named after Mayan ruin sites. Streets are named by groups of, for example, sea animals, land animals, and flowers. The streets downtown (bordered by Tulum, Cobá, Yaxchilán, and Uxmal avenues) have names of flowers, such as *Tulipanes, Crisantemas,* and *Rosas.*

A peculiarity of Cancún is the abundance of U-shaped streets called *retornos* (returns), R. for short. Take R. Tulipanes Street, for example. It starts off as Tulum, goes around the block, and ends again in Tulum, one short block from where it started. *Retornos,* in other words, are not drive-through streets. To drive from Tulum Avenue to Yaxchilán Avenue, which run parallel to each other, you have to take a connecting avenue, such as Cobá or Uxmal. When driving around, be careful as you approach the turnarounds on Tulum, Yaxchilán, and other avenues. Watch out for the curves 2 kilometers south of the Convention Center toward the Sheraton Hotel. They are sharp and unmarked.

Hotel Canto   *Corner of Yaxchilán and Sun Yax Chen.* Double, 1,100 pesos. 14 rooms. Tel. 30490.

Hotel Rivemar   *Avenida Tulum #49.* Double, 1,100 pesos. Phone in rooms. Tel. 30833.

Hotel Marrufo   *Avenidas Yaxchilán and Rosas.* Double, 1,100 pesos. Refrigerator in rooms, inside parking. Tel. 30480.

Hotel Yaxchilán   *Avenida Yaxchilán #41.* Double, 1,150 pesos. Inside parking. Tel. 30572.

Hotel Soberanis   *Avenida Cobá #7.* Double, 1,150 pesos. Restaurant. Tel. 30109.

Hotel Cotty   *Avenida Uxmal #44.* Double, 1,200 pesos. Inside parking, TV. Tel. 30540.

Hotel Villa Rossana *Avenida Yaxchilán #68.* Double, 1,200 pesos. A bit run-down.

Hotel Komvaser *Avenida Yaxchilán #15.* Double, 1,300 pesos. Small pool.

Hotel Hacienda Cancún *Avenida Sun Yax Chen #39.* Double, 1,400 pesos. Inside parking, some rooms have kitchenettes. Very new. Tel. 30552.

Hotel Tulum *Avenida Tulum #41.* Double, 1,450 pesos. Phone in rooms, very new. Tel. 30503.

For the money and services offered, the following hotels offer the best deal in this price range in downtown Cancún:

Hotel Plaza Caribe *Avenidas Tulum and Uxmal.* Double, 1,600 pesos. Gardens, swimming pool, restaurant, snack bar, bar, phone in rooms. Tel. 30777.

Hotel Cancún Handall *Avenida Tulum.* Double, 1,700 pesos. Swimming pool, phone in rooms, indoor parking. Very new. Tel. 30972.

Hotel El Parador *Avenida Tulum #26.* Double, 1,800 pesos. Phone in rooms, indoor parking, gardens. Tel. 30584.

Hotel Plaza del Sol *Avenida Yaxchilán #31.* Double, 2,000 pesos. Phone in rooms, swimming pool, patio, restaurant, bar, indoor parking. Tel. 30888.

HOTEL ZONE

All the hotels in the hotel zone have their own beaches, one or more restaurants, bars and swimming pools, shops and gardens. Some have travel and car rental agencies. Naturally, the more expensive they are, the more services and comforts they offer. In fact, a couple of the most expensive hotels have Sunday Masses held in their grounds.

The only exception to the rule is the **CREA Youth Hostel,** Kukulkán at km 3. It is the cheapest place for single travelers to stay in Cancún. There are 650 comfortable bunk beds divided into separate sections for women and men. There is a bar, dining room, swimming pool, and beach. The rate is 350 pesos per person.

───────────────── **DELUXE** ─────────────────

Club Verano Beat Hotel   Double, 4,000 pesos.

Hotel Playa Blanca   Double, 5,000 pesos.

Hotel Bojorquez   Double, 3,500 pesos.

Hotel Carrousel   Double, 7,000 pesos.

Hotel Calinda   Double, 3,500 pesos.

Casa Maya Hotel   Double, 7,000 pesos.

Hotel Club Lagoon   Double, 6,000 pesos.

Hotel Maya Caribe   Double, 3,500 pesos.

Hotel Dos Playas Inn   Double, 2,500 pesos.

Hotel El Presidente   Double, 8,000 pesos.

Hotel Cancún Viva   Double, 4,500 pesos.

Fiesta Americana   Double, 8,000 pesos.

Camino Real   Double, 8,000 pesos.

Hotel Aristos Cancún   Double, 4,000 pesos.

Hotel Hyatt Cancún   Double, 7,500 pesos.

Hotel Cancún Sheraton   Double, 8,000 pesos.

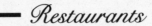

Restaurants

───────────────── **DOWNTOWN** ─────────────────

Most restaurants in downtown Cancún are located either on Avenida Tulum and its side streets, or on Avenida Yaxchilán (4 short blocks east of Tulum and parallel to it). The restaurants in the Avenida Tulum area offer cooking styles, dishes, and prices to please every palate and pocket. The dishes and the atmosphere are definitely more Mexican in the restaurants on Avenida Yaxchilán. A number of budget restaurants can be found on Avenida Uxmal off Tulum. They offer similar menus of meat, chicken, pork, and seafood dinners that cost approximately 100 pesos.

Hotel restaurants in the hotel zone are not included in this listing.

Restaurant La Barca   Lunch and dinner specials for 150 pesos. A la carte lunch approximately 300 pesos.

Restaurant Valladolid   Same as above.

Restaurant Leonardo   *Calle Margaritas.* Lunch specials 150 pesos. A la carte lunches and dinners 200 pesos.

Restaurant Maruca   Lunch and dinner specials between 100 and 150 pesos.

Restaurant Mexico   *Tulipanes #22.* Mexican food. Lunch specials (after 1:00 P.M.) 150 pesos. A la carte dinners under 200 pesos. Good food and good service. Open 7:00 A.M. to 10:00 P.M.

Dan's Hamburgers   *Tulum and Claveles.* Hamburgers, hot dogs. Superburger 150 pesos. Self-service. Outdoor tables.

Restaurant Cafetería Pop   *Tulum #26 (next to Hotel Parador).* An American-style cafeteria serving American-style foods. Lunch specials and a la carte dinners approximately 200 pesos. Closed Sundays.

Restaurant El Palenque   *Cobá #4 (corner of Tulum).* Mexican dishes and seafood. The menu is limited, but it offers original dishes such as stuffed steak. Dinner approximately 300 pesos.

Restaurant El Pescador   *Tulipanes #5.* International and Mexican seafood. Good food, excellent service, and pleasant atmosphere. Dinners approximately 400 pesos. Lobster 700 pesos. Wine list. Open 7:00 A.M. to 11:00 P.M.

The Happy Lobster   *Tulum #63.* Seafood and American-style steaks. Dinner approximately 250 pesos. One of the more popular sidewalk restaurants on Avenida Tulum. Open 8:00 A.M. to 11:00 P.M.

The Lobster House   *Tulum and Claveles.* Seafood. Similar menu prices and setting to the Happy Lobster.

Gypsy's Restaurant   *Azucenas #15.* Oriental-style seafood. Very limited menu including tempura and lobster in various styles. Patio dining, wine list. Dinner approximately 500 pesos.

Black Beard's Taberna *Tulum #29.* Seafood and meats. Another of Avenida Tulum's popular sidewalk restaurants. Specialties: charcoal-grilled seafood and meat brochettes. Lobster, various styles, approximately 700 pesos. Dinner approximately 500 pesos. Open 8:00 A.M. to 11:00 P.M.

Choko's Lobster House *Claveles (a half block from Tulum).* Ample menu of seafood and Mexican food. House specialties: conch ceviche, seafood soup, and red snapper Choko's. Wine list. Large and busy, but service is prompt. Dinner approximately 500 pesos. Open for lunch. Tel. 30319.

Restaurant Augustus Caesar *Claveles #33 (a block from Tulum).* Italian food. House specialties: spaghetti *frutta di mare,* shrimp-stuffed ravioli. Ample menu of pasta, meat, poultry, and seafood. Italian and Mexican wines, full bar. Very good, authentic Italian cuisine. Budget dinners approximately 350 pesos. Open 1:00 P.M. to 2:00 A.M. Tel. 20240.

Most of the restaurants in Avenida Yaxchilán are located on two small blocks between Avenidas Sun Yax Chen and Uxmal. You could take a short walk past them, check them out, and make your choice.

Many restaurants here stay open until 4:00 in the morning.

Tacos D.F. *Yaxchilán and Sun Yax Chen.* The best and cheapest lunch spot in Cancún. Tacos are prepared with tortillas made right in front of you, and cost 25 pesos apiece. (Three or four tacos satisfy the average appetite.) Open 10:00 A.M. to 2:00 P.M.

The following restaurants specialize in charcoal-grilled beef tacos; chicken, pork, chorizo, bacon, and other tacos, *quesadillas,* and Mexican clay-pot fondues. They are busy and lively and serve good food, but they are not ideal for quiet dinners.

Los Parados *Yaxchilán #35.* Taco dinner 250 pesos. Serves beer.

Restaurant La Parrilla *Yaxchilán #51.* Taco dinner 250 pesos. Serves beer.

Grillo's *Yaxchilán #41.* Taco dinner 250 pesos. Also specializes in brochettes. Serves beer.

For full-course dinners in a quieter atmosphere, try the following restaurants:

La Fogata *Yaxchilán #67.* Charcoal-grilled meat and chicken dishes, plus an ample menu of typical Mexican dishes. Dinner approximately 250 pesos.

Restaurant Bar Los Arcos *Yaxchilán #32.* Seafood Mexican style. Original house specialties. Outdoor tables. Dinner approximately 450 pesos. Open 1:00 P.M. to 3:00 A.M.

Perico's Restaurant Bar *Yaxchilán #71.* Mexican seafood, charcoal-grilled meat, and other popular Mexican specialties. The best Mexican décor and atmosphere in Cancún. Dinner approximately 500 pesos.

Other restaurants in Yaxchilán:

Pizzas Sorrento *Yaxchilán and Sun Yax Chen.* Medium-size pizzas 200 pesos. A couple of pasta dishes. Wine by the glass.

Restaurant Cruji-Pollo *Yaxchilán and Sun Yax Chen.* A Kentucky-fried-chicken type of restaurant. Quarter chicken 100 pesos, half 160, whole 350 pesos. Also serves fries and sandwiches.

La Tasca Restaurant Bar *Yaxchilán #82.* Cancún's only Spanish restaurant. Serving typical Spanish dishes such as paella, *fabada,* and gazpacho. Paella dinner (big enough for two) and pitcher of sangría 500 pesos. Open 6:00 P.M. to 4:00 A.M.

Restaurant El Potrero *Yaxchilán #51.* Steak house. Charcoal-grilled American steaks. Sonora State meats. Dinner approximately 500 pesos.

———————— RESTAURANTS ON CANCÚN ISLAND ————————

Charcoal Broiled Burgers *Hotel Verano Beat.* Burger, salad, and glass of beer 250 pesos. Open 4:00 P.M. to midnight.

Tucan Tarr *Convention Center.* Hamburgers, tacos, fruit, and seafood cocktails. Breakfasts and some dinner dishes. Lunch approximately 200 pesos, dinner under 400 pesos. Open 8:00 A.M. to 11:00 P.M.

Augustus Pizza *Convention Center.* Pizzas, salads, breakfasts. Dinner 350 pesos (small pizza, a salad, beer or wine.) All open-air tables.

Restaurant-Bar Tik-Tak *Kukulkán Boulevard at km 5.5 (in front of Vacation Clubs International).* American-style restaurant and cafeteria. Soups, salads, sandwiches, Mexican dishes, breakfasts. Lunch and dinner approximately 400 pesos.

Restaurant Casa Rolandi *Plaza Caracol (next to the Convention Center).* Wood-oven pizzas, homemade pastas, Italian-style seafood and meat dishes. Pizza lunch 250 pesos. Dinners approximately 400 pesos.

Gypsy's Pampered Pirate *Kukulkán Boulevard at km 12.* Restaurant-bar. Mostly seafood, some meat dishes. Limited menu, good food. A quiet romantic spot by the Nichupté Lagoon. Dinner approximately 350 pesos.

Carlos 'N Charlie's *Kukulkán Boulevard at km 5.5.* This restaurant's formula for success is good food served with large side orders of humor and craziness. Varied menu of beef, pork, chicken, and fish. Dinner approximately 600 pesos.

Some of the hotel zone's fancy restaurants are:

Cancún 1900 *Convention Center.* International cuisine.

The Compass Rose *Convention Center.* Mongolian smoke-oven specialties.

Mauna Loa Restaurant *Convention Center.* Mandarin and Cantonese cuisines.

 *Nightlife*

The heart of every old Mexican city is the main plaza. There, by day or by night, one can watch the city's life and activity and feel its pulse as people flow into it to do business, to stroll around, and to socialize in its outdoor cafés. In Cancún no one really knows where it is and not much happens. Avenida Tulum is the heart of the city, and the local nightlife starts there and moves on to bars and discotheques throughout the city as the night progresses.

Begin your evening out by dining in one of the numerous restaurants on Avenida Tulum and its side streets, or in Avenida Yaxchilán's restaurant area.

Guests of hotels in the hotel zone often do not need to leave the grounds of these minitowns to look for excitement. A guest there could, for example, have a before-dinner drink in one of the hotel's bars, walk a few steps to have dinner in one of its restaurants, and then dance the night away in its discotheque. Outside of the restaurants, bars, and discotheques in the hotels, there is a good selection of restaurants and night spots scattered throughout the hotel zone.

The Convention Center has a concentration of restaurants where you can dine anywhere from the simple outdoor setting of Augustus Pizza to the elegant atmosphere of gourmet restaurants such as Cancún 1900 and the Mauna Loa. Quiet, isolated restaurants can be found here and there along Kukulkán Boulevard (see "Romantic Spots," page 92).

If you don't want a place with a quiet little table in the corner, then you will fit right into the beehive atmosphere of Carlos 'N Charlie's.

For disco dancing try the **Bum Bum Bar** at the Hotel El Presidente, Tuesday through Sunday, 9:00 P.M. to 2:00 A.M. Bake and shake to the hot tropical rhythms of *cumbia* and *salsa* played by the Cancún Brass Band. The Bum Bum (pronounced Boom Boom) has no cover and no minimum and most mixed drinks are under 170 pesos. Beer is 80 pesos.

The Lone Star Bar, Avenida Yaxchilán, next to Hotel María de Lourdes, is Cancún's only country-western wateringhole offering a couple of deals to its thirsty patrons: a free margarita at happy hour on Sunday, Tuesday, and Thursday from 8:00 to 10:00 P.M. and free welcome cocktails for groups of 12 and over, if they call first. No cover, no minimum. Beers are 80 pesos and Mexican mixed drinks are 150 pesos.

Other discotheques include **Cocay** at the Hyatt Cancún Hotel, open daily from 9:00 P.M. to 4:00 A.M., cover, Sunday through Thursday, 175 pesos, Friday and Saturday 225; **Krakatoa,** Convention Center, open daily 11:30 P.M. to 5:00 A.M., cover 125 pesos; and **The Mine Co.,** Hotel Verano Beat, open daily 11:00 P.M. to 5:00 A.M., cover 125 pesos.

---------- **ROMANTIC SPOTS** ----------

Vitamins, proteins, and carbohydrates are all good for you, but there are times when a good ration of passion is all your body needs. Cancún's beaches are beautiful at night. The temperature is a pleasant 70 degrees, the breeze is soft and fresh, and the sky is clear. Most beaches then are deserted and there are plenty of private spots to lie back and count the stars.

For romantic dinner spots try one of the following restaurants. **The Club Lagoon Hotel** has an elegant, yet unpretentious restaurant where dinner is served by candlelight. The food is good and the prices are reasonable. **The Palapa Bar,** also at the Club Lagoon, is a quiet bar overlooking the Nichupté Lagoon. It has soft dance music, and you can even bring your favorite cassette—the bartender will be more than happy to play it for you. **Gypsy's Pampered Pirate** (km 12, Kukulkán Boulevard) is a small, quiet restaurant overlooking the lagoon.

Beaches and Activities

You have worked hard all year and more than earned your vacation. Now all you want is a beach where you can lie in the warm sun, read a chapter of the most recent best-seller, take a nap, wake up, take a splash, drink a piña colada, get sleepy, take a nap, and so on until it is time to go to bed.

Cancún's beautiful beaches lend themselves perfectly to this kind of relaxation and laziness without guilt. (If guilt symptoms appear, double the dose of relaxation and take frequent naps.) Soft, fine sand carpets the long, wide beaches of Cancún—the same sugarlike sand that many absentminded vacationers have mistakenly used to sweeten their coffee. It won't do that, but it will cushion your body into many sweet dreams.

All the beaches in Cancún are located on the seaward side of Cancún Island, along Kukulkán Boulevard. City buses from downtown Cancún service all beaches as far as the Hotel Cancún Sheraton at km 13. The beaches on the Bahía de Mujeres side of Cancún Island (from the CREA Hostel, km 3 to Hotel Cancún Viva at km 8) are generally calm and protected from sea currents and strong waves. On the Caribbean side, from Punta Cancún to Punta Nizúc, the beaches face the open sea and have waves up to 3 feet high. Some beach areas have a strong undertow. Take the following precautions before getting in the water:

1. Ask hotels about swimming conditions on their beaches.
2. Check tide and undertow warnings posted at most hotels. The absence of warning signs does not necessarily indicate safe swimming conditions.
3. Do not swim where there is no lifeguard.
4. Do not swim alone.
5. When in doubt about swimming conditions, stay out.

All beaches, including those in front of fancy residences and hotels, are public. Signs placed along Cancún's beaches by Sectur (the Mexican Tourism Ministry) establish this clearly: "The beaches of Mexico are public. No one can prohibit the access and free transit through them and in the 60-foot strip next to sea."

However, hotels provide rest rooms, showers, towels, etc. only for their own guests. There are a few city beaches that may be used by guests of hotels downtown. Most have parking space and refreshment stands, but none has lifeguards, rest rooms, or showers.

Playa Linda, Km 5, Kukulkán Boulevard, is located by the Nichupté Bridge, behind the Zona Naval barracks. Playa Linda ("Pretty Beach") is a large desolate beach with no shade or facilities. The water is clear and there are no waves. Do not swim or snorkel on the Nichupté Canal side of Playa Linda. The current and the small-boat traffic there make it unsafe.

Playa Tortugas, Km 7, Kukulkán Boulevard, is marked with a large sign that reads *Playa Recreativa* and is right next door to Hotel Dos Playas Inn. The water here is clearer and deeper than in Playa Linda. The waves are about a foot high and there is no undertow or current. There is a long *palapa* for shade and a bar where soft drinks are 50 pesos.

Playa Chacmool, Km 10, Kukulkán Boulevard, between Aristos and Playa Sol hotels, is a typical Cancún beach, with beautiful sand and turquoise water. The first 40 feet of water are less than knee-high in depth and ideal for children (at least those above knee-high). Past this point the water gets gradually deeper. The sea here can get rough on stormy days. Check the tide warning sign a few yards south of the restaurant on the beach. The small *palapa* restaurant at Chacmool sells tortas, soft drinks, beer, and coconuts at reasonable prices.

South of the Sheraton Hotel, Km 13, Kukulkán Boulevard (200 yards south of the entrance), there is a path to the beach through the vegetation. From this point to Punta Nizúc, 6 miles south, there are no hotels (at present). This is the only stretch of more or less desolate beach to be found in Cancún. There is no bus service south of the Sheraton.

––––––––––––––––––––––– **CAMPING** –––––––––––––––––––––––

Cancún does not have a single campground or trailer park, and considering its orientation toward high-rise, high-priced hotels, it may never have one. Eight km (5 miles) from Cancún, though, is Camping de Gante, the peninsula's best campground. (See Punta Sam section, page 62.) The large parking lot next to Playa Linda, km 4 at Kukulkán Boulevard, can be used by recreational vehicles for overnight stays. It is far enough from the boulevard, quiet, and has no buildings, hotels, or houses around it. No one you could disturb and no one to disturb you.

––––––––––––––––––––––– **DEEP-SEA FISHING** –––––––––––––––––––––––

Cancún, like Cozumel, offers a large selection of deep-sea fishing operators, boats, and rates. Fishing arrangements can be made for half- or full-day trips. In both cases, tackle and bait are included in the price. Lunch is included only on full-day trips. Make your reservations a couple of days in advance.

Club de Pesca Pez Vela *Km 5.5 Kukulkán.* Five 25- to 42-foot boats with 2 to 4 chairs and lines. Full-day charge is 6,875 to 9,000 pesos. Tel. 30992.

Cancún Avioturismo *Km 5.5 Kukulkán.* Four 24-foot boats with 2 chairs and 4 lines with 2 outriggers. Full-day charge is 9,075 pesos. Tel. 30325.

Marina Playa Blanca *Playa Blanca Hotel.* Six 30- to 42-foot boats with 2 to 4 chairs and lines. Full-day charge is 7,250 to 8,250 pesos. Tel. 30606.

Water World *Km 6 Kukulkán.* Four 29-foot boats with 2 chairs and 4 lines with 2 outriggers. Full-day charge is 7,500 pesos. Tel. 30554.

Aqua Tours *Km 6.5 Kukulkán.* Four 19- to 36-foot boats with 2 to

4 chairs and lines. Full-day charge is 5,800 to 11,250 pesos. Tel. 30227.

Mauna Loa Marina *Convention Center.* One 24-foot and two 23-foot boats with 2 chairs and lines each. Full-day charge is 8,250 to 9,375 pesos.

──────────────── **SHORE FISHING** ────────────────

The Nichupté Lagoon is teeming with fish and often, from its edges, you can see barracudas, jacks, and needlefish among others. But here is the catch—the bottom of the lagoon is shallow, thick with algae, and there are few spots where shore fishing is possible.

The Nichupté Canal, under the bridge of the same name, is located at km 4 of Kukulkán Boulevard. Try casting with spoons, one ounce or less, for jacks and other fish, or try bait fishing when the current is not too strong.

The Sigfrido Canal branches off the Nichupté Canal and runs parallel to Kukulkán Boulevard in front of the Calinda Hotel. The water here is clear enough that you can see the spots where the fish are. Also try spoons or bait. As you probably know, sunset is a good time for fishing. Here it is a good time for leaving, otherwise you will become the bait of huge schools of mosquitoes.

On the Caribbean Sea side of Cancún Island you will need a good casting rod and about one-ounce spoons and other lures to try your luck for blue runners, bar jacks, and other jacks.

──────────────── **SAILING** ────────────────

Sunfish and Hobiecats are the only sailboats available for rent in Cancún. Although all marinas quoted only hourly rates, they are often willing to make discounts for daily rentals. In Cancún marinas are windsurfer, Hobiecat, and Sunfish rental places. In some cases, marinas are beach stands renting entire fleets of diving masks, snorkeling equipment, and fins.

Wind Surfing School Center *Hotel Bojorquez.* Rates are 250 (Sunfish) and 500 (Hobiecat) pesos per hour. Instruction costs 500 pesos.

Marina El Presidente *Hotel El Presidente.* Rate is 225 pesos per hour for a Sunfish.

Club de Vela Casa Maya *Casa Maya Hotel.* Rates are 200 (Sunfish) and 500 (Hobiecat) pesos per hour.

Club Lagoon Hotel Rates are 175 (Sunfish) and 400 (Hobiecat) pesos per hour.

Aqua Quin *Camino Real Hotel.* Rates are 375 (Sunfish) and 500 (Hobiecat) pesos per hour.

Marina Playa Blanca *Playa Blanca Hotel.* Rates are 150 (Sunfish) and 450 (Hobiecat) pesos per hour.

Marina Bojorquez *Hotel Bojorquez.* Rate is 500 pesos per hour for a Hobiecat.

─────────────── **SCUBA DIVING** ───────────────

Cancún's reefs are as beautiful and full of sea life as any of the reefs in Mexico's share of the Caribbean Sea. However, with maximum depths of 40 feet, they are rather shallow in comparison to many of the reef areas south of here, and don't compare to Cozumel's spectacular drop-offs. Cancún's diving services are limited, but adequate to the demand there is for them.

Chital Reef is one mile north of Hotel El Presidente in Cancún's hotel zone. It has a maximum depth of 16 feet (4 feet to coral tops). This is the shallowest reef in the bay and a great one for snorkeling. It consists of two long, narrow sections, running from east to west. The longer section is 600 yards long by 35 yards wide. The shorter one is 350 by 25 yards. The main sights in this elk-horn coral reef are gray-and-yellow-tail snappers, blue tangs, blue chromis, and lots of large barracudas.

Maximum visibility 100 feet. One knot current. Anchor dive.

Cuevones Reef (*cuevones* means "small caves" in Spanish) is surrounded by about 10 small caves, the longest of which is 18 feet long. The others are between 6 and 10 feet long. The maximum depth here is 35 feet, and 20 feet to the top of the coral.

The reef is only 2 miles north of Punta Cancún and is made up of a combination of rock, elk-horn, and brain coral. It consists of two strips running from east to west. The bigger one is 250 yards long by 40 yards wide, while the smaller one is 100 yards long by only 10 yards wide.

Cuevones has a large population of reef fish with numerous

schools of snappers, groupers, amberjack, and barracuda. Nurse sharks are at times found on the reef's bottom or in the caves.

Maximum summer visibility is 150 feet, around 60 feet in winter. Two-to-three-knot current. Reef dive.

Manchones Reef is located 5 miles northeast of Cancún and only 2 miles south of Isla Mujeres. It runs southeast to west and is 300 yards long by 150 yards wide. The reef's average depth is approximately 35 feet and 15 feet from the surface to the coral tops. The absence of currents, ample visibility, shallow depths, and abundance of sea life makes Manchones good for beginners.

Manchones is formed mostly of elk-horn and brain coral.

Water temperatures 65 to 75 degrees. Maximum visibility 190 feet. Anchor dive.

La Bandera Reef is the smallest of the four reefs found in Bahía de Mujeres, yet it has the largest reef-fish population of them all. I have seen here more midnight and blue parrotfish and larger schools of porkfish and grunts than in any other reef in the area. Consequently, such quantities of reef fish attract numerous predators such as jurels, yellow jacks, and barracudas, and the reef is always boiling with activity.

La Bandera is 4 miles northeast of Punta Cancún. It consists of two sections, one 150 yards long by 25 yards wide and the other 100 yards long by 50 yards wide.

The reef is made up of elk-horn and brain coral, and like Cuevones Reef, it has a few small caves. The maximum depth is 36 feet, and 16 feet to the coral tops.

Maximum visibility 130 feet. Two-and-a-half-to-three-knot current. Reef dive.

Punta Nizúc, a deeper and more challenging reef, is located 8 miles south of Cancún. This reef is actually the beginning of a reef that stretches all the way down to Honduras in Central America.

Neptuno Dive Shop (NAUI) *Club Verano Beat Hotel, Km 3 Kukulkán.* 30 aluminum tanks, Mako 7 CFM compressor, two 23-foot Fish Nautique boats, 2-tank day, instruction costs 1,750 pesos for 3-hour resort course. Tel. 30772.

Water World (PADI) *Km 6 Kukulkán.* 50 steel tanks, Mako 12 CFM compressor, four 27-foot Phoenix boats, 2-tank day, instruction costs 1,625 pesos for 3-hour PADI resort course. Tel. 30554.

SNORKELING

The ideal habitat for most tropical fish is rocks, coral reefs, and even shipwrecks. Here they can find their food, hide from predators, live, and reproduce. Cancún's sandy, rockless beaches are a poor habitat for rock beauties, mahogany snappers, bicolor damselfish, and dozens of other species of colorful tropical fish. Nevertheless, these very same beaches provide a fantastic habitat for tanned beauties, burnt-back beach nappers, and other sun lovers.

Chital Reef and **Cuevones** and **Manchones reefs** are for experienced snorkelers.

Chital is located about a mile north of Cancún Island. With depths between 4 and 16 feet, this is Cancún's best snorkeling reef. Cuevones and Manchones reefs are located between Cancún and Isla Mujeres. Both are diving reefs, but their shallow depths (30 to 40 feet) also make them good snorkeling spots.

Water World (Tel. 30554) and Neptuno Divers (Tel. 30772) take snorkelers along on their scuba-diving trips to Chital, Cuevones, and Manchones. The rate is 375 pesos, including equipment.

Guided boat tours to **Garrafón** (Isla Mujeres) are basically snorkeling tours for intermediate and beginning snorkelers, although they are not promoted as such. For details, see "Guided Boat Tours" (Cancún), page 100. Most tour fares to Garrafón include equipment. **Xelhá** is also a prime snorkeling spot accessible on guided tours.

Equipment rentals are available at Cancún's dive shops, beach stands in the hotel zone, and at Garrafón and Xelhá. Day rentals run between 100 and 200 pesos.

WATERSKIING

There are two waterskiing areas in Cancún. The **Nichupté Lagoon,** with its smooth surface is Cancún's favorite waterskiing area, and the northern side of Cancún Island is also a good waterskiing area, except on very windy days, when the water gets choppy. Equipment can be rented at the following locations.

Club Lagoon Hotel   Rates are 650 pesos per hour and 300 pesos per hour for instruction. Tel. 31111.

Mauna Loa Marina   The rate is 800 pesos per hour.

Marina Cancún Viva   Rates are 800 pesos per hour and 300 pesos per hour for instruction.

WIND SURFING

A wind surfer is a small sail mounted on a surfboard, and wind surfing is the solution to surfing without surf and sailing without a sailboat. Try wind surfing when you visit Cancún. All you need is a little muscle, a good sense of balance, and a couple of hours of instruction.

Club de Vela Casa Maya *Casa Maya Hotel.* Rates are 150 pesos per hour and 500 pesos for a 2-hour course.

Playa Blanca Wind Surfing *Playa Blanca Hotel.* Rates are 200 pesos per hour and 750 pesos for a 3-hour course.

Wind Surfing School Center *Hotel Bojorquez.* Rates are 200 pesos per hour and 500 pesos for a 2-hour course.

Marina El Presidente *Hotel El Presidente.* Rates are 225 pesos per hour and 1,000 pesos for a 3-hour course.

Club Lagoon Hotel Rates are 150 pesos per hour and 1,000 pesos for a 3-hour course.

Aqua Quin *Camino Real Hotel.* Rates are 200 pesos per hour and 450 pesos for a 1$^1/_2$-hour course.

Tours

Cancún is an ideal location for guided or independent day tours. For instance, the ruins of Chichén Itzá are two hours' driving time and the ruins of Tulum are one hour's driving time from here; the national park of Xelhá and a good half-dozen hidden beaches are an hour away; and tiny Isla Mujeres is only a 40-minute boat ride from Cancún.

For guided-tour tickets you may contact any of the travel agencies listed at the end of this section. Fare prices do not include 10 percent tax.

Independent tours are a cheaper alternative to guided tours where everything is organized for you, if, however, you don't consider it a hassle to take buses and discover places on your own.

Before you leave on a guided tour or one of your own creation, be sure to take sunscreen, sunglasses, and a hat or scarf for your head.

GUIDED BOAT TOURS

The tiny national park of Garrafón in Isla Mujeres is the most popular destination for boat day tours from Cancún. With its clear water and hundreds of colorful, cracker-eating tropical fish, Garrafón is one of the best snorkeling spots in the Cancún–Isla Mujeres area. The cruise to Garrafón is made by boats ranging in size from 35 to 300 passengers and the tour prices run between 350 and 750 pesos. None.of these tours includes a stop in the town of Isla Mujeres.

Aqua Quin **Trimaran**   Leaves daily at 10:30 A.M. from the Camino Real Hotel. Tel. 30100. Stops at Manchones Reef for 45 minutes, then continues on to Garrafón where it stays for 2 hours. Fare includes two drinks, lunch, and snorkeling gear. Adults 675 pesos, children 500 pesos. Returns by 4:00 P.M.

Don Diego **Trimaran**   Departures daily at 11:00 A.M. from the Playa Blanca Hotel marina. Tel. 30606. The *Don Diego* is a 47-foot fiberglass trimaran with capacity for 45 passengers. It stops first at Garrafón for an hour of snorkeling, then continues to Playa Lancheros for a look at the turtle pens. After lunch, if the wind is favorable, the boat sails back to Cancún, and just before the end of the trip, the crew gives a demonstration of spinnaker flying. The price of the tour includes open bar, lunch, and snorkeling gear. Adults 750 pesos; children under 12, 650 pesos.

Manta **Trimaran**   Departures daily at 11:00 A.M. from Hotel Bojorquez marina. Tel. 30072. One way to snorkel without even getting in the water is to take a trip on this glass-bottom trimaran. The *Manta* stops at Garrafón for snorkeling and lunch. Adults 650 pesos; children under 15, 450 pesos.

Fiesta Maya **Yacht**   This superyacht leaves Tuesday through Sunday at 10:00 A.M. from the marina across the street from Hotel El Presidente. Tel. 30389. The *Fiesta Maya* has a maximum capacity of 300 passengers, but it usually leaves with about 200. It is the most economical of the boats going on this tour. The fare includes two drinks but no lunch. Snorkeling equipment is available for rent on board for the one-hour stop at Garrafón.

The *Fiesta Maya* has a snack bar, full bar, boutique, glass bottom, and live tropical music group. Tickets are valid for any day. Adults 350 pesos.

——— GARRAFÓN AND ISLA MUJERES ON YOUR OWN ———

1. Take the bus to Puerto Juárez on Avenida Tulum. They run about every 15 minutes (fare 6 pesos).

2. Take a passenger boat from here to Isla Mujeres. (See Isla Mujeres passenger boat schedule.) Fare 50 pesos.

3. Take a taxi to Garrafón at the pier in Isla. The fare is 150 pesos for up to 5 passengers (or walk, it's 5 kilometers to Garrafón).

4. Admission to Garrafón, 10 pesos.

5. Snorkeling gear rental, 75 pesos.

6. You can have lunch at Garrafón for approximately 300 pesos. Approximate round-trip cost: 750 pesos.

On your return trip, take a walk around the town of Isla Mujeres. It is nice and small and quite different from Cancún.

————————— GUIDED TOURS OF RUINS —————————

These tours are conducted daily by English-speaking guides in comfortable air-conditioned buses. In most cases, tour buses will pick you up at your hotel and drop you off there at the end of the tour. The rates for these tours are the same at all travel agencies.

Chichén Itzá The tour costs 760 pesos plus 15 percent tax; includes lunch, and leaves at 8:15 A.M. and returns by 6:00 P.M. The ruins of Chichén Itzá are among the largest and most impressive archaeological sites in the Yucatán Peninsula. If you only have time to visit one archaeological site while in Cancún, make it Chichén Itzá.

Tulum/Xelhá/Playa del Carmen The tour costs 640 pesos plus 15 percent tax; includes lunch, and leaves at 8:15 A.M. and returns by 4:30 P.M.

Tulum is a small but spectacular Mayan site built on a cliff by the turquoise water of the Caribbean Sea. Xelhá National Park is a clear-water lagoon with an immense variety of tropical fish. Snorkeling conditions are ideal here. There are no waves or currents, visibility is approximately 50 feet in most areas of the lagoon, and the maximum water depth is 10 feet. Akumal is a beach resort set in a shady coconut grove. Snorkeling is also good there. Playa del Carmen, a growing beach town, serves as the terminal for passenger ferries to Cozumel.

───────── **TOURS OF THE RUINS ON YOUR OWN** ─────────

In Cancún the central bus station (Central de Autobuses) is located at Avenidas Tulum and Uxmal. It is advisable to buy your bus ticket the night before your trip.

Chichén Itzá Buses to Mérida via Chichén Itzá leave every two hours starting at 6:00 A.M. Many buses do not stop at Chichén Itzá, but stop instead at the town of Pisté, one mile west of the ruins. The bus fare is 200 pesos. Admission to the ruins is 15 pesos (10 pesos on Sunday). To take the return bus to Cancún, it is best to walk to Pisté's main square. Buses always stop here if they have room. Additionally, Pisté has a number of budget restaurants serving lunch plates for about 200 pesos. Approximate round-trip cost: 600 pesos.

Tulum/Xelhá/Akumal These points are south of Cancún on the main highway. Akumal is 65 miles, Xelhá 70 miles, and Tulum 80 miles from Cancún.

1. Buses to these destinations leave about every hour from Cancún. The bus fare to Tulum is 160 pesos.
2. Get off at the junction to Ruinas de Tulum, *not* at Pueblo Tulum, 3 miles past the ruins.
3. Walk a mile from the main highway to the ruins.
4. Admission to the ruins is 15 pesos (10 on Sunday).
5. At the entrance to the ruins, there are a number of restaurants with lunch plates for about 300 pesos. Approximate round-trip cost: 600 pesos (visiting Tulum only).

Limit your tour to two places (Tulum and Xelhá, for example, as they are next to each other). That way you will not spend a good part of the day waiting for buses. Remember, if you miss a bus, it takes about an hour for the next one to come by.

Do not leave from these points later than 7:00 P.M. After this time, buses are either too full to stop or simply do not stop. Friday, Saturday, and Sunday afternoon are particularly bad times to catch buses back to Cancún. You can always try hitching while you wait for the bus.

ℐ to ℤ

AIRLINES

Aeromexico Main Office: *Avenida Tulum #3.* Tel. 30361. Airport: Tel. 30478.

Aerocaribe *Avenidas Tulum and Uxmal.* Tel. 30394.

Aerocozumel Airport: Tel. 30175.

Continental Airlines Airport: Tel. 31973.

Eastern Airlines *Convention Center.* Tel. 30133.

Mexicana Main Office: *Avenida Uxmal #10.* Tel. 30659.

United Airlines *Convention Center.* Tel. 30099.

AIRPORT

The international airport is located 20 km south of downtown Cancún. Services include money exchange booth, restaurant, bar, and car rental agencies.

Collective taxis to the hotel zone or to downtown hotels charge 150 pesos per person. Taxi tickets can be bought at a booth next to the car rental agencies. The Ruta 3–Bonfil–Aeropuerto bus line connects the airport with downtown Cancún.

BANKS

Bancomer and Banamex are located on Avenida Tulum on the opposite side to all the restaurants and shops. There is also a bank at the Convention Center. Banking hours are 9:00 A.M. to 1:30 P.M., Monday through Friday.

BUS STATION

The Cancún bus station is located right downtown on the tiny block at the junction of Avenidas Tulum and Uxmal. Local and through buses leave for Mérida and Chetumal and intermediate points throughout the day.

BUTCHER SHOP

Super Carnicería Cancún *Avenida Sun Yax Chen #52.* Open 7:30 A.M. to 5:30 P.M. daily. You might be glad to know where to find a good butcher shop after you have been camping and eating fish for a couple of weeks. American-style cuts.

CAR RENTALS

Daily rental rates can vary between agencies from a few to as much as 130 pesos for the same car model. There is a 15 percent tax on all car rentals so shopping around for the best deal can save you quite a bit of money. Insurance costs an additional 250 pesos. There is a big demand for rental cars at Christmastime. To secure a car for that busy holiday period, make reservations through American car rental agencies with a branch in Cancún. Be sure to take your car reservation number with you.

Avis *Hotel Cancún Viva.* Tel. 30803. Airport: Tel. 30097.

Budget *Avenidas Uxmal and Tulum.* Tel. 30961.

Cave Auto Rent *Hotel Plaza del Sol.* Tel. 30888.

Econorent *Hotel America (downtown).* Tel. 31500. Airport: Tel. 30861.

Fast *Quetzal Building.* Tel. 31650.

Holiday Tel. 30827.

Hertz Tel. 30938.

National *Camino Real Hotel.* Tel. 30373. Airport: Tel. 30142.

Quick Tel. 30181.

Rapsa Tel. 30161.

Rentautos Kankun Tel. 30137.

Xelhá Tel. 31334.

GOLF

The 18-hole Pok-Ta-Pok golf course was designed by Robert Trent Jones. For information about playing, call 30871 in Cancún.

LAUNDROMATS

Lavandería Automatica *Yaxchilán and Sun Yax Chen.* Do your own laundry or leave it. 85 pesos per load. Open 10:00 A.M. to 8:00 P.M.

Alborada *Avenida Nader #5* (behind San Francisco store on Tulum). Laundry service and self-service. Open 9:00 A.M. to 8:00 P.M.

MARKETS

There are two markets in Cancún: **Mercado Municipal** and **Javier Rojo Gomez.** Mercado Municipal is the largest, best-supplied market in Cancún and is located 6 blocks north of the bus station on Avenida Tulum. Shop before 1:00 P.M. when there is a larger selection of vegetables, fruit, and meat.

Javier Rojo Gomez is located behind the post and telegraph office at Avenida Sun Yax Chen. The selection of produce and fruit here is limited, but it is less crowded than Mercado Municipal.

MEDICAL SERVICES

The hotels in the hotel zone have their own house doctors or can recommend doctors in downtown Cancún. Budget travelers may try the **Centro de Salud** (Public Health Center), where fees are minimal and services are limited.

The Public Health Center is located at R. 4 Crisantemas, half a block from Tulum. Hours: 8:00 A.M. to 2:00 P.M. and 4:00 P.M. to 8:00 P.M. Doctors' visits are 20 pesos. Doctors here may or may not speak English, so don't come here if you have a complicated medical problem.

Hospital Central de Cirugía, Claveles #14 and Tulum (Tel. 30773 and 30882), is a private institution with general practitioners and specialists. Some doctors here speak English.

POST AND TELEGRAPH OFFICE

The post and telegraph office is located at Avenidas Sun Yax Chen and Xelhá. Open 9:00 A.M. to noon and 3:00 P.M. to 6:00 P.M., Monday through Friday, and 9:00 A.M. to noon on Saturday.

SERVI-BAR

Servi-Bars are the tiny refrigerators found in most hotels around and above the 2,000-peso range. The liquors, wines, mixers, juices, and snacks you will find in them are not included in the price of the room.

SHOPPING

Handcrafts from all corners of Mexico can be bought at the craft market on Avenida Tulum and at the craft shops in the Convention Center. Hammocks, *guayaberas, huipiles,* and black coral jewelry are among the best buys, as they are made in the peninsula.

Quintana Roo State is a duty-free zone and Mexican shoppers find a number of imported items here at lower prices than in the rest of Mexico. Americans, however, will find few bargains; on the other hand, you will find your favorite brand of peanut butter, bourbon, toothpaste, and many more American items that will give you temporary relief from homesickness.

TELEGRAPH OFFICE

See "Post and Telegraph Office."

TELEPHONE OFFICE

The long-distance telephone office is located at Azucenas and Tulum. Open 9:00 A.M. to 9:00 P.M.

TRAVEL AGENCIES

These travel agencies have organized day trips to the ruins.

Algema Tours   *Hotel Maya Caribe.* Tel. 30006.

Amecaribe   *Avenidas Tulum and Azulenas.* Tel. 30899.

Betanzos   *Ave. Yaxchilán #8.* Tel. 30399.

Cancún Holidays   *Quetzal Building.* Tel. 30161.

Expresso Mexicano   *Hotel Cancún Caribe.* Tel. 30046.

Intermar Caribe   *Hotel Cancún Sheraton.* Tel. 31288. *Hotel El Presidente.* Tel. 30970.

Rutas del Mayab   *Punta Petempich #24.* Tel. 30244.

Turitransportes Mexicanos   *Yaxchilán #3* (downtown). Tel. 30474.

Viajes Bojorquez   *Hotel Bojorquez.* Tel. 30567.

Viajes Lisina   *Quetzal Building.* Tel. 31238.

Viajes del Sureste   *Hotel Aristos Cancún.* Tel. 30684.

Wagons-Lits Mexicana   *Camino Real Hotel.* Tel. 30100.

WHITE GAS

White gas for camping stoves is a difficult item to find outside Cancún. Try Ferretería Briceño, located in front of the Pemex gas station, at the junction of Avenida Tulum and the Puerto Juárez Highway, or Tlapalería El Candado, Sun Yax Chen #56.

Beaches South of Cancún to Boca Paila

The area between Cancún and Boca Paila, 153 km (95 miles) to the south, is a long necklace of turquoise beaches. All these beaches have the same crystal-clear water, the same powdery white sand, the shade of coconut groves, the sun to warm you, and the breeze to cool you, and yet no two of them are alike. Some are great for snorkeling and diving, some for fishing, others for beachcombing. Others provide a great combination of these activities. But there is one thing they are all great for: loafing and tanning.

The only towns of any size between Cancún and Tulum are Puerto Morelos and Playa del Carmen, each one with a population of approximately 2,000 inhabitants. The stores in these towns are small and badly stocked, and at times even staples such as bread, cheese, and eggs are scarce. Campers are advised to stock up on food and water in Cancún.

The accommodations south of Cancún are an assortment of free and paying campgrounds, budget and moderate tourist-class hotels.

The kilometer count on the highway starts at Chetumal, the capital of Quintana Roo State, and ends at Cancún km 360. Most points in this section are located at the end of a one-to-two-mile offshoot of the main highway.

Gas stations can be found at Puerto Morelos, km 328 (32 km south of Cancún) and Tulum Ruins Junction, km 232 (128 km south of Cancún).

Puerto Morelos

Km 328 (32 km south of Cancún)

Two types of people go to Puerto Morelos—those who want to dive or snorkel on its beautiful reef and those who want to take the car ferry to Cozumel. Apart from this, Puerto Morelos doesn't have much to offer to visitors. The accommodations are very limited and the beach is not as nice as others south of here.

Getting There

Buses going north and south stop in Puerto Morelos approximately every hour.

Vehicle Ferry to Cozumel The ferry terminal is located 600 yards south of the main plaza. The Cozumel ferry has capacity for about 40 trucks and cars. It leaves Tuesday through Sunday, but Thursdays and Fridays are dedicated exclusively to "black cargo"—trucks carrying gas, gasoline, and other inflammables; this leaves Tuesday, Wednesday, Saturday, and Sunday for all other vehicles. Tickets are on sale from 6:00 to 7:00 A.M., loading time is 7:00 A.M., and departure time is 8:00 A.M.

Tickets are valid only for the day they are sold. To make sure you get on the ferry, get your car in line between 5:30 and 6:00 A.M., and buy your car and passenger tickets at 6:00 A.M. (have your car's license number with you).

Fares: Passengers 80, cars and pickups 325, cars and pickups with small trailer 490, buses 520, two-axle trucks 650, and motorcycles 100 pesos.

Soft drinks, coffee, and sandwiches are sold on the ferry's passenger deck. The ride to Cozumel takes 2 hours and is sometimes rocky, so come prepared with Dramamine for motion sickness.

Where to Stay

BUDGET

Posada Amor *One block south of main plaza.* Double, 500 pesos. Ceiling fans, hot water. Posada Amor (the Love Inn) is a small, 6-room family-run hotel. It also offers hammock lodging at 100 pesos per person and a small tent-camping space, 50 pesos per person.

DELUXE

Hotel Playa Ojo de Agua *One block north of the main plaza.* Double, 3,400 pesos (includes meals). Beach cabañas with ceiling fans, hot water. Playa Ojo de Agua caters to diving groups and offers special food-lodging-diving packages. For information and reservations, contact Playa Ojo de Agua, P.O. Box 1281, Suc. "A," Mérida, Yucatán, Mexico.

Restaurants

Casa Martin *Main plaza in front of the water tower.* Offers a limited menu of mostly seafood and a couple of beef and chicken dishes. Ocean soup, fish dish, and beer for 350 pesos.

Restaurant Doña Zenaida *Main plaza.* Has the best and most ample menu in town. Most dishes cost under 250 pesos. Lunch specials for 90 pesos.

Restaurant Posada Amor *One block south of main plaza.* The best home cooking in the region: *chiles rellenos, mole poblano, pollo à la cacerola,* and other Mexican dishes for under 250 pesos. Pleasant atmosphere. It is worth a detour from the main highway. Open 8:00 A.M. to 4:00 P.M. and 7:00 to 9:00 P.M.

Beaches and Activities

FISHING

The wooden pier off the main plaza is a good spot to catch a few tasty *chac-chi* for dinner. *Chac-chi* is Mayan for "red mouth" and is the name of the red-mouthed fish of the grunt family.

Fishing arrangements for reef trolling for barracuda and bottom fishing for groupers and snappers can be made at the Ojo de Agua Dive Shop. Make reservations several days in advance.

SNORKELING

It's a long 600-yard swim from the shore to the reef and there isn't much to see between. The best way to get to the reef is to go on one of the snorkeling trips available in Puerto Morelos. Ojo de Agua Dive Shop offers half-day snorkeling trips for 300 pesos per person with a 5-person minimum. Posada Amor also has a half-day snorkeling trip for 350 pesos per person, including equipment.

SCUBA DIVING

Ojo de Agua Dive Shop *P.O. Box 1281, Suc. "A," Mérida.* 31 steel tanks, Mako 7.5 CFM compressor, two 24-foot Proline boats, 900 pesos for 2 tanks, lunch not included, no instruction available.

The reef in front of Puerto Morelos starts at Punta Nizúc, 13 miles north of Puerto Morelos, and ends around the ferry terminal on the south edge of town. Another reef starts at Punta Brava, 2 miles south of the ferry terminal. The reef is 600 yards offshore and the waves can be seen breaking over the coral tops, creating a wide, foamy-white line that runs parallel to the beach for miles. In the area in front of Puerto Morelos, the reef is between 80 and 120 feet wide. The beauty and the sights of this huge reef are enough to leave you breathless; one of them is the Sleeping Shark Caves, located 8 kilometers east of Puerto Morelos. But divers who do not wish to become nervous wrecks may instead wish to dive the wreck of the Spanish galleon located 7 kilometers northeast of town. The ship's cannons can be seen at a depth of 15 feet. The average depth of the inside part of the reef is approximately 10 feet, ideal for snorkeling. On the Caribbean side, depths are greater as the sea bottom gradually drops.

The visibility throughout the reef is in the 40- to 60-foot range.

$\mathcal{A}$ to $\mathcal{Z}$

BANK

The first bank in Puerto Morelos opened in March 1982.

BUSES

Most buses running between Chetumal and Cancún stop at Puerto Morelos about every 2 hours.

GROCERY STORES

Cheese, ham, bread, eggs, and a few vegetables and fruits can be found in the three grocery stores here.

LONG DISTANCE

The long-distance office is located 300 yards south of the military camp. Open 8:00 A.M. to 1:00 P.M. and 4:00 to 7:30 P.M.

Punta Bete

Km 298 (50 km south of Cancún)
Km 296 (60 km south of Cancún)

Nothing makes a beach more tropical and exotic than the slender, graceful presence of coconut trees. Punta Bete is crowded with tall, shady coconut trees that swing and sway to the cool rhythms of the Caribbean breeze and wind ensemble. Punta Bete is a quiet, uncrowded beach with comfortable, reasonably priced accommodations that maintain high standards of cleanliness and service.

Getting There

Taxis at Cancún's international airport charge approximately 1,200 pesos for the ride to Cabañas Lafitte, Kai Luum, and Marlin Azul. Ask a couple of taxis for their rates and take the cheapest. Taxi from Playa del Carmen is 300 pesos.

Where to Stay

Cabañas Lafitte During the eighteenth century the famous pirate Jean Lafitte prowled the Caribbean's waters in search of treasures from gold-laden Spanish galleons. According to legend, many treasures are still waiting to be unearthed in these deserted beaches.

You needn't dig too deep if you are looking for a treasure of golden sunshine, turquoise waters, silk sands, comfort, quiet, and privacy without the pirate prices of some beach hotels. Cabañas Lafitte offers rustic and modern beachfront cabins, restaurant, bar, swimming pool, and game room. All cabins are built separately to allow for maximum privacy and have individual bathrooms with hot water, ceiling fans, and double or king-size beds. There is a full-service restaurant offering daily lunch and dinner specials or a la carte service. Meal prices are: breakfast, 150 to 250 pesos; lunch, 150 to 300 pesos; and dinner, 300 to 500 pesos.

A hotel is as good as the service offered by the people who manage and work in it. Lafitte's manager, Jorge Fuentes, his wife, and staff are among the most friendly and helpful people you could meet in the Yucatán Peninsula. The service and attention they provide is simply the best.

The rates (without meals) are 1,500 pesos for a single, 1,700 pesos for a double, and 2,000 pesos for a triple, plus 15 percent tax. For reservations write (in the United States) to Camptel Ventures, Inc., P.O. Box 32794, San Jose, California 95152, Tel. (408) 262-5460, or (in Mexico) to Jaime Lubcke, Calle 58 #471, P.O. Box 1463, Mérida, Yucatán, Mexico (Tel. 30485).

Kai Luum Camptel is a new concept in camping. Imagine yourself getting ready for a beach camping trip. You pack the suntan lotion, snorkeling set, swimsuit, toothbrush, and that's it. "Oh, yeah?" you say, "what about the tent, the sleeping bag, the cooking kit, etc.?" Forget all that. Kai Luum is camping for lazy campers. You do the camping and they do the work.

Your accommodations will be in room-size tents, shaded and cooled by a *palapa* roof (they are called *tentalapas* here) and in the morning your foam bed will be made by a maid. There is no need for sponge baths and no tiptoeing through the bushes either. Kai Luum has clean, separate communal rest rooms and showers with hot and cold water. And while you play or lie in the sun, good food will be prepared for you by Kai Luum's Mayan kitchen staff.

Kai Luum's restaurant offers lunch and dinner specials consisting of an appetizer, soup, main course, dessert, and coffee. The menu changes every day and there is never a dull meal here.

Meals cost approximately $15 a day for breakfast, lunch, and dinner, and $11.50 a day for breakfast and dinner only. Kai Luum's bar works on the honor system.

The rates are $22.50 for a single, $11.25 for a double, and $7.50 for a triple. Rates are per person, with 3-person maximum in a tent. For reservations write to Camptel Ventures, Inc., P.O. Box 32794, San Jose, California 95152, Tel. (408) 262-5460 or (800) 538-6898.

Note: Kai Luum and Cabañas Lafitte do not serve conch or turtle dishes as a gesture of concern for these endangered species.

Cabañas Marlin Azul   Like Lafitte, this is a small, secluded, and quiet beach hotel with its own charm and personality. There are 15 beachfront modern cabañas with ceiling fans and individual bathrooms with hot and cold water. The rate for double occupancy is 1,700 pesos.

Marlin Azul has a small restaurant with a limited selection, but the emphasis here is on quality not quantity. The red snapper à la veracruzana is the best I have ever tasted.

The costs of meals are breakfast, 150 to 250 pesos; lunch, 150 to 300 pesos; and dinner, 250 to 400 pesos.

For reservations write to Cabañas Marlin Azul, Calle 61 #477, Mérida, Yucatán, Mexico (Tel. 17410).

Xcalacoco Campground   Xcalacoco (pronounced "Shkalacoco") means twin coconut trees. It is one of the three clean and well-kept campgrounds found between Cancún and Tulum (80 miles south of Cancún). Located on the beach in a somewhat sparse coconut grove, the campground is seldom so full that you would have to camp in the full sun. Xcalacoco is large enough for about 20 pickup-sized campers without overcrowding, but outside of heavy holiday periods there are usually no more than 10 campers here.

There are five small *palapas* scattered around the camp that serve as eating, reading, or socializing areas. Fires are not allowed.

The campground's ample water supply comes from two nearby wells, and the locals use it as their drinking water. But from well to mouth there is always a chance of something getting in the water. Don't look for shortcuts; boil your water.

The rest rooms and showers are very clean. Xcalacoco also has 3 cabins with individual bathrooms. They rent for 1,000 pesos a unit, but are no bargain at that price. There is no electricity. The camping rate is 100 pesos per person per day.

Beaches and Activities

The beach at Punta Bete is a wide strip of fine, white sand edged by a coconut grove. The water is generally calm and the waves do not exceed 2 feet in height in good weather.

In some stretches the sea bottom is very rocky at the water's edge. The clarity of the water makes it easy to see that the bright turquoise areas indicate a sandy bottom, while the dark blue areas indicate a rocky bottom. Avoid entering the water in the turbid seaweed area between Cabañas Lafitte and Blue Marlin. Dips, sharp rocks, and sea urchins make it hazardous to your feet.

The four accommodations here are spread over a one-and-a-half-mile area of Punta Bete, and there are plenty of deserted beaches north and south of here. From Cabañas Lafitte, Kai Luum is about a half mile to the north. Blue Marlin and Xcalacoco campgrounds are three-quarters of a mile south.

SNORKELING

The sea bottom along the beach between Kai Luum and Xcalacoco is a mixture of large areas of either sand, rock, and coral or seaweed. As I said, the turquoise areas indicate a sandy bottom, while the dark blue ones indicate a rocky bottom. The best snorkeling is in the rocky areas once you swim 30 yards or more offshore.

Avoid swimming and snorkeling in the seaweed areas right next to shore. Hidden among the seaweed are sharp rocks and occasionally sea urchins. Inexperienced snorkelers should not snorkel alone on these beaches.

The water visibility at the beach at Kai Luum improves gradually as you swim away from the beach. Between 50 and 100 yards from the beach, visibility is approximately 50 feet. The average depth is 12 feet and the rather flat rocks at the bottom are the home of many small reef fish.

The beach at **Marlin Azul** has many sharp-rock areas. Find a sandy spot to get in the water and keep it in sight as you snorkel, so you can get out of the water the same way you got in.

If you have to get out of the water through the rocks, keep your swimming fins on (they will protect your feet from scratches), walk backward so you will not trip on the tip of the fins, and try to keep your balance so you will not end up falling (ouch!) on a sharp rock. The visibility around here is 40 feet almost right off the beach. The average depth is 10 feet. Look for schools of grunts and other small reef fish hiding in crevices and holes on the rocky bottom. There is a slight current flowing south about 25 yards offshore.

Lafitte Reef is located 300 yards offshore in front of Kai Luum Camptel. It can be reached with the reef shuttle at Kai Luum for 120 pesos an hour, or with Lafitte's own boat (if you are a guest there). The reef is shaped like a horseshoe, with its ends pointing toward the shore. It is made up of large and small patches of elk- and reindeer-horn and brain corals. Blue-striped and white grunts, gray snappers, blueheads, blue tangs, and bar jacks are some of the main inhabitants of this reef. Visibility is about 90 feet on a good day, and the average depth is 10 feet any day. Mask, fins, and snorkel rent for 125 pesos a day at Kai Luum.

Barrrrrracuda—Coming Soon

With movies like *Jaws* and *Piranha*, Hollywood has contributed a great deal to people's fears of animals, and it's actually surprising that *Barrrrrracuda* hasn't yet been filmed.

Barracudas are common reef fish. They can be identified by their fierce-looking appearance: toothy snouts, protruding lower jaws, and four or more black spots on their silvery sides. Barracudas are very curious fish and will appear out of no-where to inspect divers and snorkelers from as close as 12 feet, only to disappear into the turquoise horizons of the reefs a few seconds later. From my experience in countless diving trips, barracudas are a harmless fish. There have been, however, reports of barracudas taking an occasional nibble at people in murky waters.

The real problem with barracudas is not so much *their* bite but *yours,* as barracuda meat has been on occasion responsible for ciguatera food poisoning (*ciguata* in Spanish). As a precaution against ciguatera food poisoning, avoid eating the meat of barracudas over 2 feet in length.

SCUBA DIVING

A full-service dive shop can be found at Cabañas Lafitte.

SHORE FISHING

Off the beach the best fishing area is to the north of Cabañas Lafitte. Along here, the rocky bottom is 50 to 100 yards from the beach; the sandy bottom in between is good for bait fishing, or your hotel's restaurant can usually give you fish scraps for bait. Ideally, you should cast your baited hook no less than 20 yards from the shore.

Fishing is fairly good here, but the fish seem to be concentrated in certain spots. If you do not catch a fish within 5 minutes after casting, don't waste time; move on down the beach 50 yards or so. Repeat this procedure until you hit the jackpot. Suddenly you will be bringing out crevelle jacks, bar jacks, horse-eye jacks, long-fin pompanos, and the best fighting fish on these beaches—bonefish.

Bonefish, by the way, are an abundant catch around here. They go for almost any bait and they in turn make good bait. The bonefish in this area weigh 3 to 4 pounds at the most, but when you catch one, you will think you have hooked a nuclear submarine—well, a tiny nuclear submarine. Bonefish are too bony to eat. Keep only what you need for bait and release the rest.

BEACH HIKING/CAMPING

The hiking distance from Punta Bete to Playa del Carmen is 4 miles on flat, sandy beach. The main attraction is a good snorkeling reef right next to the beach, 3 miles south from starting point.

The shoreline between Punta Bete and Playa del Carmen is a succession of 6 bow-shaped bays each measuring a mile or less in length. Start from the point of the bay that begins a few yards south of Xcalacoco. Going south from the Xcalacoco point, the beach is typical of the terrain you will find throughout the entire hike—flat and without rocks, brush, or other obstacles. Wear sandals or walking shoes, as there are plenty of thin-bristled coral pieces and dead spiny sea urchins washed ashore.

Don't expect to find the variety of shells and birds that other beaches of the region have, but at the same time don't overlook the beautiful shell called a sunrise tellin or miss the sight of a great white heron standing on the beach a hundred yards away. You can't miss the small bands of plovers that will often accompany you on your hikes.

When you reach the end of the first bay, you will have walked about three-quarters of a mile from this point; you can see the point of the second bay, about three-quarters of a mile to the south. Halfway down this second bay is an abandoned house, where, if it is still uninhabited, you could take a break in the shade. This abandoned house looks fairly new, has a cement floor and a sand fire pit in the middle of it. The dry well next to the house is probably the reason it is abandoned. From the abandoned house it is about a mile and a quarter to the reef. The reef is at the end of the third bay and is easy to spot as the coral tops stick up about a foot from the water. Olivaceous cormorants and brown pelicans are often seen standing on the coral tops. The water visibility at the reef is about 60 feet and the depth on the side facing the beach is 8 feet or less. The reef is about 50 yards off the beach and runs parallel to it. It is about 400 yards long by about 50 yards wide. A very slight current runs between the reef and the beach. The side of the reef facing the beach is ideal for beginning snorkelers. The sea side of it, on the other hand, can get rough, and should be approached with caution. From the reef to Playa del Carmen is about three-quarters of a mile.

Nightlife

One hopes you did not come to Punta Bete expecting to find wild nightclubs and discos. If the disco bug gets you one night and you have transportation, Cancún has the medicine you need and is only 40 minutes away from Punta Bete.

The nightlife in Punta Bete consists of quiet dinners, socializing with the people you meet at your hotel, a game of pool or Ping-Pong (if you are staying at Lafitte), and quiet beach walks. Kai Luum, Cabañas Lafitte, and Marlin Azul are at a reasonable walking distance from each other. From Lafitte, Kai Luum is a half mile to the north and Marlin Azul is about three-quarters of a mile south.

You can dine at one of the neighboring hotels. (Carry a flashlight.) The restaurant at Kai Luum, for instance, is a beautiful *palapa* with rustic charm. At night, dinner is served under the light of a hundred candles and the setting looks like an altar to the jolly gods of good food. (Nonguests should make reservations.) After dinner, a quiet walk along the moonlit beach . . . and what better nightlife could one want?

Playa del Carmen

Km 287 (69 km south of Cancún)

Playa del Carmen, a small beach town with a population of 2,000 people, serves as the ferry terminal for passenger ferries to Cozumel. The town does not hold much attraction for tourists, but its beautiful beach is a good reason to visit. In fact, if you are looking for a small, not too touristy town, Playa del Carmen might just be your kind of place. Another good reason for staying at Playa del Carmen is its accessibility to nearby attractions. By bus, Xelhá National Park and the ruins of Tulum are 20 minutes south and Cancún is 50 minutes north; Cozumel is an hour away by boat.

Getting There

Bus Buses north to Cancún and south to Akumal, Xelhá, Tulum, and Chetumal go through Playa del Carmen every hour or so.

Passenger Ferry

Playa del Carmen to Cozumel	Cozumel to Playa del Carmen
6:00 A.M.	4:00 A.M.
10:00 A.M.	7:00 A.M.
noon	9:30 A.M.
2:30 P.M.	1:00 P.M.
6:00 P.M.	4:00 P.M.

Note: the car ferry for Cozumel leaves from Puerto Morelos, 31 km north of Playa del Carmen.

Airplane Aerocozumel operates 50 small-plane flights daily between Playa del Carmen and Cozumel. There are no reservations; simply show up at the Playa del Carmen airport between 6:00 A.M. and 5:00 P.M. The airport is on the southern edge of town, 5 blocks from the main plaza. The one-way fare is 250 pesos.

Where to Stay

─── BUDGET ───

Posada Lily   *One block from main plaza.* Double, 600 pesos. Hot water, ceiling fans, clean. Has parking space in front of rooms.

Motel Playa del Carmen   *Two blocks from main plaza.* Double, 750 pesos. Hot water, ceiling fans, clean. Has some parking spaces, but is not a motel.

─── MODERATE ───

Hotel Molcas   *At the ferry pier.* Double, 2,500 pesos plus tax. Air conditioning, restaurant, bar, swimming pool, Astroturf lawn.

Hotel Balam Ha   *On the beach by the pier.* Double, 2,800 pesos. Air conditioning, restaurant, bar. Has some rooms with direct access to the beach. Playa's newest hotel.

Restaurants

Playa del Carmen's inexpensive restaurants have two or three daily specials, consisting of fried fish, a meat dish, and a chicken dish, for approximately 200 pesos. Four of the inexpensive restaurants are located in the immediate vicinity of the main plaza.

Hotel Molcas Restaurant   *At the pier.* This is the only restaurant in town offering a varied menu of meats, poultry, seafood, soups, and more. It is air-conditioned, very clean, and has good service. The seafood brochette and the Yucatán-style pork chops are among its specialties. Lunch costs approximately 350 pesos, dinner 450.

Hotel Balam Ha Restaurant   *At the pier.* This restaurant's atmosphere and view make up for its limited selection. The dinner menu includes soup, your choice of main course (seafood, Mexican, or international dish), dessert, and coffee. Dinner costs 500 pesos.

Beaches and Activities

Playa del Carmen has a beautiful beach, although it is somewhat unkempt. The waves are 2 feet high or less and the beach has a gentle grade. There is usually a fresh breeze in the 5- to 8-mile-an-hour range. The beach in front of town usually does not have more than 20 to 50 people, but a 10-minute walk north or south of here will take you to very private stretches of sand.

CAMPING

There are two small campgrounds in Playa del Carmen, but they look more like crowded parking lots. In high season, you are better off camping somewhere else. Both campgrounds are on the beach.

La Ruina   From the main square, go north 1 block and turn right.

This is the better of the two campgrounds. It is clean, has one cold-water shower, and a more or less clean rest room. It has capacity for 6 pickup-sized campers. There is also a small *palapa* with hammocks for rent for backpack campers. The camping rate is 50 pesos per person per day.

Brisa del Mar   From the main square go north 2 blocks and turn right.

This tiny campground has capacity for 4 pickup-sized vehicles. The rest room is always filthy, the shower is a can with holes in it, and to make things worse, there is often not a drop of water for days. The camping rate is 25 pesos per person, 25 pesos per car.

There are many clear beach spaces about 4 blocks north of these two campgrounds. They have no facilities, but they are shady and offer plenty of elbow room. Backpack campers wishing to camp on an isolated, lonely beach should read the Punta Bete "Beach Hiking/Camping" section.

SNORKELING

Water visibility off the beach at Playa del Carmen is zilch. There is, however, a great little reef three-quarters of a mile north of here along the beach. See Punta Bete "Beach Hiking/Camping" for details on the reef.

The Molcas Dive Shop offers a snorkeling tour to Xcaret for 580 pesos per person. The tour's price includes snorkeling equipment, snacks, and two soft drinks or beers. The tour lasts 5 hours.

SCUBA DIVING

Molcas Dive Shop   25 aluminum tanks, Mako 9.2 CFM compressor, 18-foot Boston whaler, 880 pesos includes 2 tanks, soft drink, and snack, instruction costs 1,000 pesos for 3-hour resort course.

SHORE FISHING

The ferry pier is the only fishing spot in Playa del Carmen and the catch is seldom good due to the noisy ferry traffic there. Surprisingly though, bonefish do not seem to mind the noise and are often the most common catch.

DEEP-SEA FISHING

Professor Pepe Salazar is a physical-education teacher whose life is totally dedicated to "schools." He spends mornings in the Playa del Carmen elementary school teaching volleyball and basketball, and afternoons diving and fishing in the numerous schools of fish found off Playa del Carmen. Pepe speaks perfect English and will take sports fishermen and divers on fishing and diving outings in his 16-foot *Sea King*. He provides tackle and bait for trolling or bottom fishing, and his rates are negotiable. You can find Pepe Salazar at the Escuela Primaría, 2 blocks from the main plaza, from 7:00 to 9:00 A.M. Monday through Friday.

The Molcas Hotel offers a half-day (5-hour) fishing trip for 2,880 pesos. They provide tackle and bait.

A to Z

BANK

Banco del Atlantico *At the ferry pier.* Open 9:00 A.M. to 1:30 P.M. Monday through Friday.

GROCERY STORES

The grocery store at Motel Playa del Carmen has the best selection of basic staples such as eggs, cheese, some cold meats, etc. A couple of other stores can be found around the plaza. A very *simpática* Mayan woman runs the best-stocked vegetable and fruit store on a corner of the main square.

LONG-DISTANCE TELEPHONE

It is located next to the vegetable stand in the main square. Open 8:00 A.M. to 1:00 P.M., 3:00 P.M. to 8:00 P.M. daily.

PARKING

As you visit Cozumel for the day, you can safely leave your car at the military camp a short block from the pier. Day rate: 25 pesos.

Cozumel

Cozumel was discovered in 1518 by Spanish conquistador Juan de Grijalva. A year later Hernán Cortés set sail from here with 11 ships and 600 men to begin the conquest of Mexico.

Before the Spanish discovered Cozumel, the Mayans made pilgrimages here to worship *Ixchel,* the goddess of fertility. The Mayans named this beautiful island *Cozumil,* meaning the island of swallows, because of the large numbers of these birds that migrate here every year.

When it's so cold up north that shivering seems as natural as breathing and goose bumps the rule rather than the exception, let your body migrate to the warm, gentle climate of Cozumel. Cozumel is Mexico's largest island and is 28 miles long by 10 miles wide. The island's only city, San Miguel de Cozumel, is located on the leeward side and has a population of 35,000.

The city's main artery is Avenida Rafael Melgar, also known as the Malecón. It runs north-south right next to the sea and its ends turn into the coastal road. The north and south hotel zones are located along the coastal road. The main plaza is located on the Malecón.

There are no buses connecting the town with the beaches. To get around, hire taxis, or rent cars or 125 cc motorcycles.

Getting There

Passenger Ferry   Playa del Carmen, the passenger ferry terminal for Cozumel, is 11 miles directly across from here. The fare is 66 pesos for adults, 33 pesos for children. Cozumel's passenger ferry terminal is in front of the main plaza.

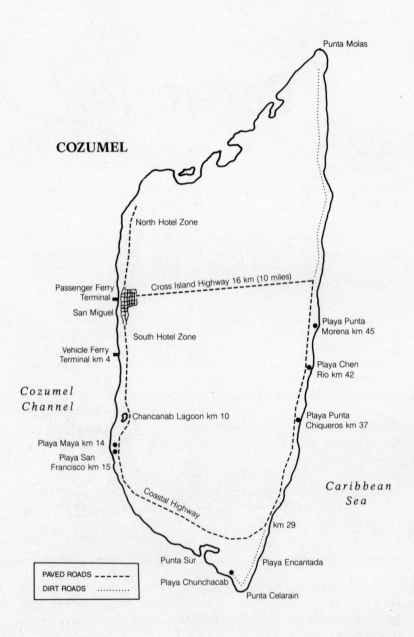

COZUMEL

Punta Molas

North Hotel Zone

Cross Island Highway 16 km (10 miles)

Passenger Ferry
Terminal

San Miguel

South Hotel Zone

Playa Punta
Morena km 45

Vehicle Ferry
Terminal km 4

Playa Chen
Rio km 42

*Cozumel
Channel*

Chancanab Lagoon km 10

Playa Punta
Chiqueros km 37

Playa Maya km 14

Playa San
Francisco km 15

*Caribbean
Sea*

Coastal Highway

km 29

Punta Sur

Playa Encantada

Playa Chunchacab

Punta Celarain

PAVED ROADS - - - - -
DIRT ROADS ·········

Cozumel to Playa del Carmen	Playa del Carmen to Cozumel
4:00 A.M.	6:00 A.M.
7:00 A.M.	10:00 A.M.
9:30 A.M.	noon
1:00 P.M.	4:30 P.M.
4:00 P.M.	6:00 P.M.

Vehicle Ferry The car ferry terminal for Cozumel is located in Puerto Morelos, 20 miles south of Cancún. (See Puerto Morelos section for detailed information.)

Departures from Cozumel to Puerto Morelos are on Tuesday, Wednesday, Saturday, and Sunday. Buy tickets from 9:00 until 10:00 A.M. Loading time is 11:30 A.M., departure time 2:00 P.M.

The car ferry terminal is 4 km south of town.

Airplane Aerocozumel's air shuttle operates 50 daily flights from Playa del Carmen to Cozumel between 6:00 A.M. and 5:00 P.M.

From Cancún there are numerous flights via Aerocaribe and Aerocozumel. For reservations on Aerocaribe, call 30394 in Cancún, 20700 in Cozumel; on Aerocozumel, call 31705 in Cancún, 20928 in Cozumel.

━━━━━ *Where to Stay* ━━━━━

Besides the hotels downtown, there are two beach hotel zones in Cozumel: the Zona Norte and the Zona Sur. The Zona Norte hotels are located between km 3 and 5 of the north coastal highway. The Zona Sur hotels are located between km 1 and 6 of the south coastal highway.

──────── **BUDGET (DOWNTOWN)** ────────

Hotel Yoly *Calle 1 Sur.* A half block from the main plaza. Double, 500 pesos. Ceiling fans, hot water. Very clean.

Hotel Flores *Calle Rosado Salas #72.* Double, 550 pesos. Ceiling fans, cold water. Friendly, family-run hotel.

Posada Letty *Calle 1 Sur #72.* Double, 650 pesos. Ceiling fans, hot water. New.

Hotel Solima *Rosado Salas #260.* Double, 650 pesos. Ceiling fans, hot water. Clean.

Hotel Pepita *Avenida 15 Sur #120.* Double, 650 pesos. Ceiling fans, hot water. Has a garden.

Hotel El Pirata *Avenida 5 Sur #3.* Double, 800 pesos. Ceiling fans, hot water. New.

Hotel Lopez *Main Plaza.* Double, 800 pesos. Ceiling fans, hot water. Another very clean hotel.

Hotel Posada Cozumel *Calle 4 Norte #3.* Double, 800 pesos. Ceiling fans, hot water. Friendly, family run hotel.

─────────────── **MODERATE** ───────────────

Hotel El Marques *Avenida 5 Sur #12.* Double, 950 pesos. Air conditioning, hot water. Very new and clean.

Hotel Elizabeth *Rosado Salas #3.* Double, 1,100 pesos. Air conditioning, hot water.

Hotel Mary Carmen *Avenida 5 Sur #4.* Double, 1,100 pesos. Air conditioning, hot water, wall-to-wall carpeting. Tel. 20356.

Hotel Bahía *Malecón #25.* Double, 1,100 pesos. Air conditioning, hot water. Some rooms with a view of the sea. Tel. 20209.

Hotel Aguilar *Calle 3 Sur #98.* Double, 1,100 pesos. Air conditioning, hot water. Pool, ample garden. Tel. 20307.

Hotel Vista del Mar *Malecón 45.* Double, 1,250 pesos. Air conditioning, hot water, rooms with sea view. Tel. 20545.

─────────────── **DELUXE** ───────────────

Hotel Colonial *Avenida 5 Sur #9.* Double, 2,000 pesos. Air conditioning, new. Tel. 20506.

─────────────── **BEACH HOTELS** ───────────────

All of Cozumel's beach hotels are in the deluxe range, and all have one or more restaurants and bars, air conditioning, swimming pool, view, hot water, and other comforts.

Hotel Cantarell *Km 3.5.* Double, 3,000 pesos.

Hotel Playa Azul *Km 4.* Double, 3,500 pesos.

Hotel El Cozumeleño *Km 4.* Double, 4,000 pesos.

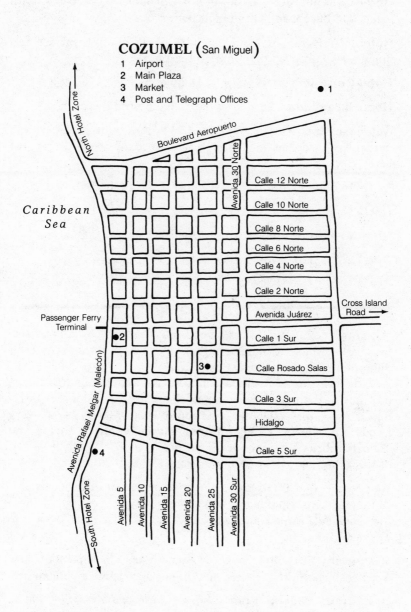

COZUMEL (San Miguel)

1 Airport
2 Main Plaza
3 Market
4 Post and Telegraph Offices

Caribbean Sea

North Hotel Zone

Boulevard Aeropuerto

Avenida 30 Norte

Calle 12 Norte
Calle 10 Norte
Calle 8 Norte
Calle 6 Norte
Calle 4 Norte
Calle 2 Norte
Avenida Juárez

Cross Island Road

Passenger Ferry Terminal

Calle 1 Sur
Calle Rosado Salas
Calle 3 Sur
Hidalgo
Calle 5 Sur

Avenida Rafael Melgar (Malecón)

South Hotel Zone

Avenida 5
Avenida 10
Avenida 15
Avenida 20
Avenida 25
Avenida 30 Sur

Hotel Cabañas del Caribe *Km 4.5.* Double, 4,000 pesos, with meals. No European plan in high season.

Hotel Mara *Km 3.* Double, 5,000 pesos, with breakfast and dinner. No European plan in high season.

Hotel Cozumel Caribe *Km 4.* Double, 5,000 pesos.

Hotel Barracuda *Km 1.* Double, 2,500 pesos. Divers' hotel.

Galapago Inn *Km 1.9.* Double, 3,000 pesos, with breakfast and lunch. No European plan in high season. Many scuba divers stay here.

La Perla Beach Hotel *Km 2.* Double, 3,500 pesos, with breakfast.

Hotel La Ceiba *Km 4.* Double, 3,500 pesos.

Hotel El Presidente Cozumel *Km 6.* Double, 4,000 pesos.

Hotel Sol Caribe *Km 3.5.* Double, 5,000 pesos.

Restaurants

Cozumel's downtown offers a good selection of Mexican and sea-food restaurants to fit all budgets. The better restaurants offer dinner entrées above the 500-peso range.

At the crossing of Avenida Benito Juárez and Avenida 10 Norte, downtown, there are several good, clean, budget restaurants serving tacos and tortas. Dinner costs approximately 80 pesos including a soda. **Lonchería el Cheef, Super Taquería, Super Tortas**, and **Tacostumbras** are open for dinner only.

All of the following restaurants have a bar.

Restaurant Las Tortugas *10 Avenida Norte.* Mexican specialties. Authentic tacos, enchiladas, *quesadillas,* melted-cheese pots. Where Mexicans eat. Dinner approximately 250 pesos. Open 7:00 P.M. to 1:00 A.M.

Restaurant El Pollo *Calle 2 Norte.* Roasted chickens and a few Yucatecán specialties. Lunch and dinner approximately 250 pesos.

Restaurant Pancho Villa *Calle 2 Norte and Avenida 5 Norte.* Mexican specialties. The front dining area is noisy and unattractive, but the back has a very pretty patio full of plants and ambience. Dinner approximately 300 pesos. Open 7:00 A.M. to midnight.

Restaurant Such Is Life *Rosado Salas and Avenida 15 Sur.* Mexican dishes and American-style sandwiches and salads. Dinner and lunch approximately 300 pesos.

Restaurant El Portal *Main Plaza and Malecón.* Mexican dishes and seafood. Ample menu. Good service. Open for breakfast, lunch, and dinner. Dinner approximately 350 pesos.

Pepe's *Avenida 5 Sur.* Mexican plates, seafood, and grilled meats and brochettes. Ample menu. Open for breakfast, lunch, and dinner. Pleasant atmosphere and excellent view of the kitchen. Dinner approximately 400 pesos.

Restaurant Las Palmeras *Main Plaza.* Ample menu of Mexican and seafood specialties. The best people-watching restaurant on the island, and also the best one to see what the food looks like before you decide to eat there. Excellent service and good food. Dinner approximately 450 pesos.

Soberanis Restaurant *Main Plaza.* Has the most ample selection of seafood on the island, but lacks atmosphere. Dinner approximately 400 pesos.

Pizza Rolandi *Rafael Melgar 22 (Malecón).* Good Italian food and pizzas served indoors or on a cool patio. Liter of house wine, 400 pesos. Dinner approximately 500 pesos.

Lone Star Texas *Malecón and Calle 10 Norte.* American-cut steaks, seafood, and Mexican dishes. Dinner approximately 450 pesos.

O Sole Mio *Avenida 5 Norte #9.* Italian food. Dinner approximately 400 pesos.

Grips' Restaurant *Malecón and Calle 10 Norte.* Seafood and meats. Dinner approximately 500 pesos.

Carlos 'N Charlie's *Malecón.* Good food and good laughs. Dinner approximately 500 pesos.

Beachcomber Restaurant *Km 9 south coastal road (Chancanab Lagoon).* This is a restaurant where you are not just an empty stomach to fill and a fat wallet to empty. The service is very personal, the food is very good, and the prices are very reasonable. House specialties include shrimp Caribe and paella. Dinner approximately 500 pesos.

Morgan's Restaurant *Main Plaza.* Seafood, meats, and chicken. Continental-style cuisine and service. Live entertainment. Dinner approximately 650 pesos.

Restaurant La Langosta *Malecón (next to Hippo's Disco).* Steaks and seafood. Limited menu of carefully prepared dishes. The only restaurant in town by the sea. Dinner 700 pesos.

Pepe's Grill *Malecón and Rosado Salas.* Steaks and seafood. Ample menu. Very pleasant atmosphere with live piano music. House specialties are beef fillet in mustard sauce and beef fillet in Roquefort sauce. Dinner approximately 700 pesos.

Nightlife

Naturally, after lying and playing in the sun all day, Cozumel's suntanned, sun-charged visitors are ready to light up the town by nightfall.

There is no better place to begin the high-voltage nightlife than at **Carlos 'N Charlie's** restaurant and bar. Watch, or take part in, the beer duels held nightly between the local locos and visiting beer guzzlers. Hutch, one of Carlos 'N Charlie's partners, can down a 12-ounce can of beer in 1.9 seconds without the slightest sign of discomfort.

Outside of Carlos 'N Charlie's, other bars downtown are nice and quiet, but not without life. The **LHY Bar,** at Calle 6 Norte and Malecón, features live Latin American *folklórica* music and is Cozumel's unofficial backgammon club. Happy hour is from 8:00 to 9:00 P.M., with two drinks for the price of one.

The **Lone Star Texas Bar,** at Malecón and Calle 10 Norte, caters to the country-western music lovers, but it lacks some of the shine of its Cancún counterpart. The bars at Hotels El Presidente, Sol Caribe, Cozumeleño, and Cabañas del Caribe are close to town and usually feature live Mexican music and a fun atmosphere.

In the high season, Cozumel's discos are boiling with as much activity as the reefs around it. The most popular places to do the scuba doo are downtown. **Hippo's Disco** is the best deal in town, as it has no cover and no minimum, except on Saturdays in high season. It also features the only video games in town.

Scaramouche Disco is the newest in town and is very popular and crowded. The cover is 70 pesos per person.

All of the discos have similar hours, 10:00 P.M. to 4:00 A.M., and drink prices: beer 80, Mexican drinks 120, and imported drinks 200 pesos.

On the quiet side of Cozumel's nightlife is the **Forum's Mexican Variety Show.** The show is a well-staged assortment of typical dances and traditional songs from Michoacán, Veracruz, Chiapas, Jalisco, and other states. Admission is 325 pesos and includes one drink. Showtime is 7:00 to 9:00 P.M. Monday through Saturday. Mexican buffet dinners are available. Tickets are valid for any day and are sold in hotels and travel agencies.

—————————————— **ROMANTIC SPOTS** ——————————————

When it's time to go to sleep but you feel like staying up and dreaming, go to one of Cozumel's dark, desolate beaches to watch the stars. But have ready a list of wishes, because on a clear night it's not unusual to see two, three, and sometimes as many falling stars as you wish.

If you have transportation, San Francisco, Chunchacab and other beaches away from town are very private and quiet at night. In town, a walk along the Malecón can be fresh and pleasant.

For a quiet, romantic dinner, with good food and soft music, nothing beats the Beachcomber Restaurant at Chancanab Lagoon.

Beaches and Activities

Cozumel's shoreline is a blend of solid stretches of either rock or sandy beach. By far the best and calmest beaches are those located on the leeward side of the island. Each one of them carries the Caribbean's trademark of golden sunshine, soft white sand, swaying coconut trees, and warm water in hues of blue and turquoise that defy description.

The access to hotel beaches here is less restricted than in Cancún. After all, when nonguests visit a hotel's beach they usually patronize its bar, restaurant, and equipment rental services. In Cozumel, however, as in all of Mexico, the 60 feet of beach next to the sea is a public area.

LEEWARD SIDE

Chancanab Lagoon   *10 km (6 miles) south of town.* This beautiful lagoon is a prime snorkeling spot and has a small sandy area for sunbathing.

Playa Maya   *14 km (8.7 miles) south of town.* A very shallow beach with a narrow strip of sand. The water is very calm and safe for swimming. There is a restaurant here.

Playa San Francisco   *15 km (9 miles) south of town.* San Francisco is the largest and most popular of Cozumel's open beaches. Like Playa Maya, the water is very shallow and safe for swimming.

In the high season, Russian and Scandinavian cruise ships anchor in Cozumel. They unload a few hundred beach-hungry tourists, and this San Francisco gets as crowded as Fisherman's Wharf or Chinatown in the other San Francisco.

There are restaurants here, offering lunch entrées in the 250-to-400-peso range.

WINDWARD SIDE

The east end of Avenida Juárez turns into the cross-island highway. Costa Oriente, as it's called here, is 16 km (10 miles) from town to the windward side of the island. There are four beaches with safe swimming areas along the eastern coast road. Swimming can be unsafe in other beach areas along this side of the island.

Playa Punta Morena   *18.5 km (11.5 miles) from town, Km marker 45.* Behind and to the right of the restaurant at this beach, there is a small protected cove where swimming and snorkeling are safe. South of this restaurant the beach is sandy for about a mile. To the north, however, it's a solid rock with razor-sharp edges.

The restaurant at Punta Morena offers a few seafood dishes. Fish fillet, for example, served with beans, rice, and a salad, is 200 pesos. Soft drinks are 30 pesos, beer 60 pesos, and mixed drinks 120 pesos. Dinner by reservation only.

The 6-room motel at the beach offers maximum quiet and privacy. The rustic rooms are equipped with kitchenettes, hammocks, and gaslight. Double, 600 pesos.

Playa Chen Río   *21.5 km (13 miles) from town, km marker 42.*

Chen Río has an attractive cove, a good stretch of sandy beach, and a large flat area that is ideal for camping. However, there are no facilities and no shade.

Playa Punta Chiqueros *26.5 km (16.5 miles) from town, km marker 37.* Punta Chiqueros is the largest of the three coves on the windward side of the island. Although the water is shallow and often a bit turbid, you can't always see the somewhat rocky bottom. Whenever you find yourself on a beach like this, it is safer to stay out, as rocks are an ideal growing medium for coral, sea urchins, and other underfoot hazards.

Playa Chunchacab *South on the Costa Oriente highway to the Punta Celerain Road, km marker 29.* Punta Celerain is the island's southern-point lighthouse. From the lighthouse, it's 1.2 miles to Playa Chunchacab over a one-lane dirt road. An ugly abandoned restaurant marks the beginning of Playa Chunchacab. Ironically, only the sea waves found it appetizing enough to frequent—and have chewed its side to pieces.

The beach here is very shallow and calm. Enter the water through the rock-free areas. There are no facilities at Chunchacab. The lighthouse keeper at Celerain sells soft drinks, coffee, fried fish, and beans and rice dishes.

──────────────── **BEACHCOMBING** ────────────────

The windward side of the island is Cozumel's best area for beach-combing. It is a large area, and it would take days to comb the entire shoreline. There are, however, two spots that can offer an especially good yield of shells: Punta Molas and Punta Celarain, the island's northernmost and southernmost points respectively.

Start your beachcombing on any of the sandy or rocky points along the shoreline. Stretches of sandy beach are also good spots; you have a better chance of finding unbroken shells in these areas than in the rocky ones. Playa Encantada, the beach stretch just before Punta Celarain, and Playa Chunchacab, for example, can offer many surprises. Among the shells you can find on Cozumel's beaches are measled cowries, sunrise tellins, sea biscuits, sea urchins, coral pieces, conches, bleeding teeth, West Indian top shells, olives, virgin nerites, incurved cap shells, cones, limpets, rough-ribbed nerites, and zebra nerites.

The best beachcombing in Cozumel, however, is at a spot I call El Cheatalittle, where you can find about 50 species of clean, shiny shells for your collection. This spot is nothing less than the local shell stand, and it is located in the craft market on the east side of the main plaza. Don Demetrio Lopez, the owner of the stand, has been collecting and selling shells and other sea objects for 25 years. He is very friendly, speaks English, and doesn't mind browsers.

─────────── BEACH HIKING/CAMPING ───────────

There are several stretches of beach along the windward side of the island that are good for beach hikes. They are found at Punta Morena, Chen Río, Punta Chiqueros, and at Playa Encantada, the beach parallel to the dirt road from km 29 of the main highway to Punta Celerain.

Playa Chunchacab to Punta Sur   A very pretty beach for a hike is Playa Chunchacab, about one mile east of the lighthouse at Punta Celerain. Even though it is very accessible, it is very deserted and has some good spots for backpack camping.

This hike starts at the abandoned restaurant at Playa Chunchacab. About a quarter mile from here, there is a tiny lagoon full of rotted seaweed. Do not cross the lagoon at its mouth. The accumulation of seaweed here is so great that it could be unsafe. The safest way to get to the other side is to proceed from where the ground is more solid.

Beyond this point, the beach is again a carpet of soft white sand, as far as Punta Sur, three-quarters of a mile from the lagoon. At Punta Sur, the vegetation merges with the sea, and it is not possible to continue the hike. This hike is 2 miles round trip.

Punta Molas   The Punta Molas dirt road begins at the end of the cross-island highway, on the windward side of the island. This is a 15-mile-long road that is passable only with motorcycles or four-wheel-drive vehicles. Because of this, very few people visit the attractive beaches found along the road.

The first beach you will find on the Punta Molas road is at km 4 (mile 2.5). If you wish to hike to it, you'll make better time walking on the road than along the rocky shoreline. This sandy beach starts at an abandoned beach house, and it is a one-mile hike to its end.

The second beach starts at the second tiny Mayan building, at km 12 (mile 7.5) and runs north for about 3 miles. In my opinion, this is the most beautiful beach in all of Cozumel, and it is superb for hiking, camping, and beachcombing.

Obviously, hiking to this beach and then back to the main highway requires a great deal of time. The best way to get there is to rent a jeep or motorcycle. Make sure, however, that the jeep you rent has traction in all four wheels, as some car rental agencies disengage the four-wheel drive.

CAMPING

There isn't a single campground in Cozumel, but there are several camping spots on the windward side of the island, via the cross-island highway. All of these are over 10 miles from town and present a transportation problem to backpack campers. There are no facilities, stores, or even a drop of fresh water in any one of these camping spots.

Windward Side Sand Road At the end of the cross-island highway, 10 miles from San Miguel, the paved road makes a 90-degree turn and continues south. This point marks the beginning of a sand road that runs north to Punta Molas, 15 miles away.

From its very first yard, this sand road is recommended only for four-wheel-drive vehicles and motorcycles. Along this road are numerous isolated camping spots right by the beach. One of the nicest, and also the closest, is a grassy, flat area next to an abandoned house, 2.6 miles from the start of the sandy road.

Chen Río Exactly 21.5 km (13 miles) from town, at km marker 42, there is a large flat area right next to the beach that can accommodate about five camping vehicles.

Chen Río to Punta Celerain's Lighthouse Between these two points, there are numerous turnoffs from the main highway that lead toward the beach; you can camp on this beach.

Playa Chunchacab See "Beaches."

SHORE FISHING

A presidential decree of June 2, 1980, prohibits commercial and sports fishing from the municipal pier, downtown, to Punta Celerain, the island's southernmost point, from the high-water mark to a depth of 50 meters offshore.

Technically, fishing is legal from the municipal pier to the northern end of the island. However, since fish and fish-watching are Cozumel's main attractions, shore fishing here is a little like hunting in a zoo.

──────────── **DEEP-SEA FISHING** ────────────

Cozumel is the home of the International Billfish Tournament, held every year during the month of May. The main categories are the Juniors' Fishing Tournament, the 30-Pound Test Fishing Tournament, the Municipal Swordfish Tournament, the Marlin and Gigantic Tuna Tournament, and the Sailfish Tournament. Reservations to participate should be made a year in advance.

During the 1980 tournament, the boat *Hooker* caught a "grand slam," consisting of one sailfish, one blue and one white marlin, and a swordfish—all in one day. This was the first known grand slam in Billfish Tournament history. For information and reservations, write to Agencía Maritima de Cozumel, P.O. Box 341, Cozumel, Q. Roo, Mexico.

Agencía Maritima de Cozumel   *P.O. Box 341.* Ten 27- to 53-foot boats with 2 chairs and 4 lines. Full-day charge is 6,250 to 13,750 pesos. Tel. 20118.

Carlotony Tours S.A.   *Hotel Bahía, Avenida Rafael E. Melgar 25.* Five 29- to 46-foot boats with 2 chairs and 4 lines. Full-day charge is 8,750 to 12,500 pesos.

Fantasia Divers   *Malecón.* One 31-foot boat with 2 chairs and 4 lines. Full-day charge is 8,500 pesos.

──────────── **SAILING** ────────────

Sociedad Cooperativa de Servicios Turisticos   *Municipal Pier.* Thirty 25- to 45-foot motor sailboats for rent.

Viajes y Deportes del Caribe   *Hotel El Presidente.* Rates here are 275 (windsurfer) and 400 (Sunfish) pesos per hour. Instruction costs 625 pesos.

──────────── **SCUBA DIVING** ────────────

There are over a dozen major reefs in Cozumel, with a range of depths and diving conditions to accommodate everyone from beginners to the most experienced and demanding divers.

Every corner, crevice, cave, and tunnel of Cozumel's spectacular reefs are teeming with an endless quantity and variety of sea life. Cozumel has some 100 species of fish alone, with colors and shades that are a treat for the eye and names that are music to the ear and stimulants to the imagination. Yellowtail damselfish, clown wrasses, rainbow parrotfish, and rock beauties are but a few of the colorful inhabitants of Cozumel's reefs.

In most reefs, visibility is 100 feet or more, but at Palancar in Cozumel, one of the world's greatest reefs, it reaches an eye-popping 250 feet. Cozumel has the best selection of diving services in the Mexican Caribbean.

La Ceiba Reef La Ceiba has set an underwater sight-seeing trail, starting by the plane wreck about 100 yards offshore. The trail is marked with signs indicating the names of various types of corals, sponges, and other reef life found in this area.

Visibility is about 120 feet and depth 55 feet.

Yocab Reef Yocab is an ideal reef for beginner divers as it is well protected from currents. It starts a short distance north of San Francisco Reef and is about 400 yards long by 30 yards wide. Yocab is a spectacular underwater garden of corals and bright-colored tropical fish.

Depth is in the 30-foot range and visibility is up to 100 feet.

San Francisco Reef This is one of Cozumel's shallower and most popular reefs. It is located one mile offshore from Playa San Francisco and is about 500 yards long. San Francisco's reef is loaded with schools of grunts, snappers, and many other fish.

Visibility is approximately 100 feet, the average depth, 50 feet.

Santa Rosa Wall The Santa Rosa Wall is located half a mile offshore, betwen Yocab and Palancar reefs. The drop-off starts at a depth of about 50 feet. There are a number of large Nassau and black groupers here that have gotten used to eating out of a diver's hands. Be careful, as this friendly "groupie" can inflict a bad bite.

Visibility is up to 200 feet. A two-knot current makes this a drift dive.

Palancar Reef This may well be the Grand Canyon of the underwater world. The spectacular wall here starts at a depth of about a mile.

Among the numerous features of Palancar's topography are caves, tunnels, gigantic coral columns, and overhangs. Palancar is located between Colombia Reef and the Santa Rosa Wall. It's one mile offshore and three miles long.

The current is up to two knots. This is a drift dive.

The visibility is up to 250 feet.

Colombia Reef Colombia Reef is located about a half mile off Punta Sur, between Maracaibo and Palancar reefs. The reef starts at a depth of about 50 feet; caves, tunnels, ravines, and coral columns are found throughout. Also common throughout the reef are vase and purple sponges, yellowtail snappers, barracuda, ocean trigger-fish, and spotted eagle rays; green turtles are seen occasionally.

A current of up to three knots makes Colombia one of the most challenging of Cozumel's reefs.

Maracaibo Reef Located about a mile off Punta Sur, the reef faces the open waters of the Caribbean Sea; it is Cozumel's most difficult reef.

Aqua Safari *P.O. Box 41.* 210 aluminum tanks, 3 Worthington 15 CFM compressors, 32-foot motor sailer, 1,100 pesos includes 2 tanks and lunch, 1,100 pesos for 3-hour resort course. Tel. 20101, 20661.

Captain Nemo's Nautilus *Chancanab Lagoon.* 25 aluminum tanks, 24-foot jet boat, 3½-hour PADI resort course.

Damselfish Divers, Inc. *Hotel Villablanca, P.O. Box 230.* 100 aluminum tanks, 2 Mako 5 CFM and 11 CFM compressors, 21-foot ski barge and 24-foot V-hull pina, 1,100 pesos includes half-day and 2 tanks, 1,100 pesos for ½-day resort course. Tel. 20730.

Deportes Acuaticos *Calle 8 Norte and Rafael Melgar.* 100 aluminum tanks, Mako 9.2 CFM compressor, 28-foot and 30-foot Yamaha outboard, 1,100 pesos for 2 tanks and lunch, 1,100 pesos includes 4-hour NAUI resort course, special dive tours to Chinchorro can be arranged.

Discover Cozumel Dive Shop *P.O. Box 75.* 150 aluminum tanks, Worthington 25 CFM and Ingersoll-Rand 15 CFM compressors, 23-foot Mako and 33-foot diesel boat, 1,100 pesos includes 2 tanks and lunch, 1,100 pesos for 3½-hour PADI resort course. Tel. 20280.

Dive Cozumel *Hotel Barracuda, Rafael Melgar, P.O. Box 163.* 160 aluminum tanks, 2 Worthington 20 CFM compressors, 35-foot motor sailer and 24-foot hydrodine, 1,100 pesos includes 2 tanks, 3-hour PADI resort course available. Tel. 20002.

Fantasia Divers *P.O. Box 176.* 160 aluminum tanks, Worthington 24 CFM and Mako 16 CFM compressors, two 36-foot flat-top trimarans, 1,100 pesos includes 2 tanks and lunch, 1,200 pesos for 5-hour PADI resort course. Tel. 20725, 20700.

Hotel La Ceiba *South Coastal Road, P.O. Box 284.* 100 aluminum tanks, Mako 15 CFM compressor, 22-foot custom boat, 1,100 pesos includes 2 tanks and lunch, 3-hour resort course available. Tel. 20730.

Scuba Cozumel *P.O. Box 289.* 120 steel tanks, 2 Worthington 15 CFM compressors, 34-foot flat-top and three 22-foot speedboats, 1,100 pesos includes 2 tanks and lunch, 1,250 pesos for 3-hour PADI resort course. Tel. 20627, 20853.

SNORKELING

Like scuba diving, snorkeling is a good enough reason for a special trip to Cozumel. There are miles of great snorkeling, right off the beach, and in many cases all you need to do is walk out of your hotel room, put on your mask, snorkel, and fins, and plunge into the turquoise sea.

The visibility throughout most of the calm leeward side of the island is between 100 and 200 feet. Snorkeling is not recommended on the rough, windward side of Cozumel.

Hotel Cantarell (Zona Norte) Snorkel among a couple of hundred Bermuda chubs and feed them from your hand. These guys are hooked on bread, tortillas, potato chips, and crackers and will eat anytime.

Hotel La Ceiba (Zona Sur) In 1977 an airplane was sunk here for the filming of a movie. Since then the plane wreck has become one of Cozumel's snorkeling and diving attractions.

The wreck is about 100 yards offshore from the dive shop at the hotel. It lies in about 40 feet of water and has become an apartment complex for such diverse tenants as four-eyed butterfly fish, mahogany snappers, blue-striped grunts, blue tangs, and other squatters.

Chancanab Lagoon Km 10, south coastal road. Chancanab is a tiny lagoon about the size of an Olympic swimming pool and is connected to the sea by a 60-yard-long cave.

Chancanab is a nice little lagoon with a few colorful fish in it, but that's just a smudge of paint. On the shoreline next to it, the sea life is so abundant that it seems as if a rainbow had shattered and fallen into the sea, becoming a myriad of multicolored fish.

Queen and stoplight parrotfish, blue-striped and white grunts, queen angelfish, yellow goatfish, peacock flounder, yellowtail damselfish, and blue tangs are some of the bits and pieces of rainbow swimming around here.

Nonswimmers can also have fun here. Just throw a piece of bread into the sea and watch the water boil when dozens of Bermuda chubs and sergeant majors come to eat it.

During my last visit here in December 1981, Chancanab was undergoing major plastic surgery to turn it from a simple, beautiful spot into a tourist center. One hopes the changes will be for the better.

Diving and snorkeling equipment at Chancanab can be obtained at Captain Nemo's Nautilus. (Tanks, 25 aluminum; boat, 14-foot jet boat [for divers]; instruction, 3$^{1}/_{2}$-hour PADI resort course, 1,000 pesos.)

Most of Cozumel's dive shops offer snorkeling tours to a couple of the shallower reefs such as San Francisco and Yocab. Depending on the shop, these tours last between 4 and 6 hours, may include lunch and snorkeling equipment, and cost between 600 and 800 pesos per person. These tours are best suited to experienced swimmers.

Mask, snorkel, and fins can be rented at most beach hotels and at dive shops downtown for approximately 100 pesos a day. Good-quality snorkeling equipment can be bought at the shops downtown and in some of the dive shops. Scuba Cozumel, for example, has a good selection of masks, snorkels, and fins selling for about 2,000 pesos a set. Snorkeling equipment is cheaper in the United States.

--------------------- **WIND SURFING** ---------------------

Aqua Sport   *Cozumel Caribe Hotel.* Rates are 200 (wind surfer) and 250 (Sunfish) pesos per hour. Instruction costs 750 pesos.

Buzos Profesionales de Caribe   *Hotel Cabañas del Caribe.* Rates are 200 pesos per hour for a windsurfer and 500 pesos for instruction.

Viajes y Deportes del Caribe   *Hotel El Presidente.* Rates here are 275 (wind surfer) and 400 (Sunfish) pesos per hour. Instruction costs 625 pesos.

Tours

There are several boat tours from Cozumel, varying in duration from one to seven hours. Guided tours of the ruins include Chichén Itzá, by boat and bus or by plane, and Tulum and Cobá, by boat and bus. Take advantage of cloudy weather for your tour of the ruins. You can't get much of a tan then, and the temperatures are a bit cooler in the interior of the peninsula.

GLASS-BOTTOM BOATS

Cooperativa de Servicios Turisticos *Municipal Pier.* This short hour-and-a-half tour leaves every 2 hours, starting at 8:00 A.M. Visits La Ceiba's plane wreck. Cost is 200 pesos per person. Tel. 20080.

Viajes y Deportes del Caribe *Hotel El Presidente.* This hour-long tour leaves from the hotel pier every hour between 10:00 A.M. and 3:00 P.M. Visits Paradise Reef. Cost is 200 pesos per person. Tel. 20923.

ROBINSON CRUSOE TOUR

The Robinson Crusoe Tours are a combination of boating, snorkeling, and a beach picnic lunch. Itineraries and destinations vary from company to company.

Aviomar *Malecón 13.* Leaves daily at 9:30 A.M. from the Cozumel Caribe Hotel and lasts 7 hours. Tour price includes lunch, soft drinks, or beer. Cost is 700 pesos per person.

Cooperativa de Servicios Turisticos *Municipal Pier.* Leaves daily at 9:30 A.M. and lasts about 7 hours. Tour price includes lunch, two soft drinks, or two beers. Cost is 500 pesos per person. Tel. 20080.

Viajes y Deportes del Caribe *Hotel El Presidente.* Leaves from the hotel pier Tuesday, Wednesday, Friday, and Sunday only at 10:00 A.M. and lasts 6 hours. Price includes lunch but not drinks. Cost is 700 pesos per person.

ISLAND TOUR

This guided bus tour of the island takes you to the Aquarium, Chancanab Lagoon, San Francisco Beach, and beaches on the windward side of the island. You'll be picked up at your hotel at 10:00 A.M. Price does not include lunch or beverages. Cost is 325 pesos per person.

──────────── **GUIDED TOURS OF RUINS** ────────────

Turismo Aviomar *Malecón 13, Chichén Itzá.* Boat and bus tours leave daily at 7:00 A.M. from the municipal pier. Cost is 1,925 pesos per person and includes guided tour of the ruins and lunch. Returns by 7:00 P.M. Airplane tours leave at 8:00 A.M. from Cozumel's airport. Cost is 2,200 pesos per person and includes guided tour of ruins but no lunch. Returns by 1:30 P.M.

Tulum-Xelhá. Boat and car tours leave daily at 9:30 A.M. from the municipal pier. Cost is 1,150 pesos per person and includes guided tour of the Tulum ruins, lunch, and a snorkeling stop at Xelhá National Park. Returns by 7:00 P.M.

Tulum-Cobá Boat and car. Leaves daily at 7:00 A.M. from the municipal pier. Costs 1,900 pesos per person and includes guided tours of both the Tulum and Cobá ruins and lunch. Returns by 7:00 P.M.

Cancún Boat and bus. Leaves daily at 9:30 A.M. from the municipal pier. Costs 1,150 pesos per person and includes a tour of Cancún's beaches and hotels. Returns by 7:00 P.M. Reserve your tour a day or two in advance during the high season.

──────────── **INDEPENDENT TOURS OF RUINS** ────────────

Independent day tours of Chichén Itzá and Cobá are difficult, not so much because of the distance but because of the bus connections and the time-consuming boat ride to and from the mainland. Tulum is a more realistic goal for an individual day tour.

1. Leave on the 7:00 or 9:30 A.M. ferry to Playa del Carmen; fare 66 pesos.

2. From there take one of the through buses to Tulum Ruins Junction. The fare is 50 pesos.

3. Admission to the ruins is 15 pesos.

4. Lunch in one of the restaurants is about 120 pesos.

5. Approximate round-trip cost: 370 pesos.

6. Be back at Playa del Carmen before 6:00 P.M. to catch the last ferry.

A to Z

AIRLINES

Aeromexico *Downtown under Cine Cozumel.* Tel. 20251.

American Airlines Airport: Tel. 20399.

Continental Airlines Airport: Tels. 20487, 20576.

Mexicana *On Malecón, 2 blocks south of Main Plaza.* Tels. 20157, 20263.

United Airlines Airport: Tel. 20408.

AIRPORT

Cozumel's airport is 2 miles from the center of town. Collective taxi fares to downtown are 35 pesos per person; to north and south hotel zones, 50 pesos per person.

AQUARIUM

Rafael Melgar and Circumvalación. The aquarium is about one-tenth of what it should be to give a good idea of the marine life around Cozumel. Admission: Adults 20 pesos; children 15 pesos.

BANKS

There are three banks on the main plaza: Banco del Atlantico, Bancomer, and Banpais. Some charge higher commissions than others. Check them before cashing your money. Open 9:00 A.M. to 1:30 P.M.

CAR RENTALS

Most rented cars in Cozumel include unlimited mileage.

Avis *Hotel El Presidente.* Tel. 20322.

Budget *Corner of 5 Avenida Norte and Calle 2 Norte.* Tel. 20903.

Rentadora Maya *Avenida Boulevard.* Tel. 20655.

Servicio Rubens *Corner of Calle 1 Sur and Avenida 10 Sur.* Tel. 20258.

CHESS AND DOMINO CLUB

El Encuentro, a small restaurant downtown on the corner of Calle 1 Sur and Avenida 10 Sur, is the town's meeting place for chess and domino fans. Playtime: after 8:00 A.M.

LAUNDRY

Lavandería Mañana, *Avenida Circumvalación, 2 blocks east of the aquarium.* Leave your laundry, 30 pesos a kilo. Open 9:00 A.M. to 6:00 P.M.

MARKET

Cozumel's well-stocked Mercado is at Avenida 20 Sur and Calle Rosado Salas. There are several budget restaurants near the entrance.

MEDICAL SERVICES

Dr. Manuel Marin-Foucher *Calle Adolfo Rosado Salas #260.* Office hours: 10:00 A.M. to 12:00 noon; 5:00 P.M. to 8:00 P.M. Tel. 20949 (office), 20912 (home). House calls.

Dr. Marcia Wiechers *Avenida 20 Norte #225.* Office hours: 8:00 A.M. to noon.

Hospital y Centro de Salud *Avenida Circumvalación* (5 blocks east of aquarium). Open 24 hours a day. Doctor's visit: 50 pesos (no house calls).

MOTORCYCLES

Small 50 and 70 cc motorcycles are available for rent in many shops in Cozumel. When renting one, make sure that it has a full tank, and that all lights, the brakes, and the horn are working. To avoid mechanical problems, rent as new a one as possible. Most shops are open from 8:00 A.M. to 8:00 P.M.

Rentadora Caribe *Rosado Salas 3.*

Rentadora Cozumel *Rosado Salas 3.*

Rentadora Leo

Discover Cozumel Dive Shop

Pancho's Rentals *Calle 2 Norte and Avenida 10 Norte.*

Servicio Ruben's

POST AND TELEGRAPH OFFICES

Both are located in the same building at the Malecón and Calle 7 Sur. Telegraph hours are Monday–Friday 9:00 A.M. to 8:30 P.M.; holidays, Saturday and Sunday, 9:00 A.M. to 1:00 P.M.

Post office hours are Monday–Friday 9:00 A.M. to 1:00 P.M.; 3:00 P.M. to 6:00 P.M.; Saturday and holidays, 9:00 A.M. to 1:00 P.M.

TAXIS

Rates within downtown: 60 pesos
Downtown to Zona Norte: 100 pesos
Downtown to Hotel Mara: 80 pesos.
Downtown to airport: 100 pesos
To airport from north or south hotel zones is 100 pesos for one person. When more than one person, add 25 percent to rates after midnight. Tels: 20236 or 20041.

TELEPHONE OFFICE

The only *larga distancia* office in town is located on the south side of the main plaza. Hours are 9:00 A.M. to 2:00 P.M.; 4:00 P.M. to 10:00 P.M.

WATER SKIING

Hotel El Presidente   550 pesos an hour.

WEATHER REPORT

Call **Discover Cozumel Dive Shop,** Tel. 20280, for the weather report.

Hidden Beaches Opposite Cozumel

PAAMUL

Km 274 (86 km south of Cancún)

A night around a campfire with newfound friends, fresh-caught fish, and fresh-bought tequila can make all the difference between one beautiful beach and another. While camping at Paamul, I met a group of Dutch people, a group of Americans, and some Canadians. At night we pooled our resources and energies to cook dinner. The Americans cooked the fish, the Canadians made a salad, and I burnt the rice while listening to the Dutch sing a ballad. We all ate the fish and nobody washed the dishes.

After that night we had dinner together several times, but we didn't always have burnt rice à la Mexicana. We also managed to have burnt rice à la American, à la Canadian, and à la Dutch.

Paamul is a tiny beach with a small hotel and camping area.

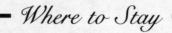

Where to Stay

BUDGET

Hotel Paamul Right on the beach. Double, 500 pesos. Ceiling fans, cold water, electric light from sunset to 10:00 P.M. Eight rooms. The camping area is on the south end of the hotel and is large enough for five vehicles. The rest room and shower are in the nearest room of the hotel. Camping rate: 50 pesos per person.

Beaches and Activities

Paamul's beach is a combination of rock and sand. The sandiest point of the beach is the southern half. The water is very shallow, and the bottom is very rocky. Sea urchins are abundant here. Avoid getting in the water where poor visibility does not allow you to see these prickly creatures.

BEACH HIKING/CAMPING

Hike length is one mile north or one mile south on a sandy beach to the north and a rocky shoreline to the south.

Bring food, water, protective clothing against the sun, head cover, sandals.

North of Paamul At the north end of the hotel there is a narrow trail through the jungle that leads to a bay about three miles larger than Paamul's. Unlike Paamul's rocky beach, the beach here is nothing but pure white sand and is private and lonely enough that you can swim in the bare minimum. This beach is only a mile from Paamul.

South of Paamul The shoreline south of Paamul is a wide strip of solid rock that can be hiked for miles. As on other beaches in the area, beachcombing is good here for coral pieces of all sizes. Among the many boulder-size pieces of brain coral that I have seen here, there was one that must have weighed 150 pounds. Coral only grows in the water, and this particular piece was a good 30 yards from the edge of the sea. I sat on this gigantic piece of brain coral and let my tiny brain ponder the strength and fury of the wave that lifted and threw such a heavy piece of coral onto the beach.

SNORKELING

The tiny bay of Paamul is protected by a reef that transforms waves into ripples. Snorkeling here is almost like snorkeling in a swimming pool (except of course on stormy days). You will need to swim 20 yards or more away from the beach before the visibility is good enough (30 feet) to see the sights and enjoy the delights of the underwater world. The depth in the first 70 yards from the shore is between 10 to 15 feet. As you get closer to the reef, 150 yards from the shore, visibility increases to around 50 feet and the depth drops to 20 to 25 feet. Naturally this reef is great for scuba diving, and divers with their own gear and compressor could have miles of reef to themselves.

YAL-KU LAGOON

Km 256.5 (104 km south of Cancún)

Yal-Ku Lagoon is Xelhá's pretty little sister without the heavy makeup and the crowds of admirers. The entrance to Yal-Ku Lagoon is an unmarked narrow dirt road, opposite a ranch house with a large stone wall and a large windmill.

Yal-Ku is only about one-tenth the size of Xelhá, but it is just as beautiful and full of fish. I have seen here, for example, more rainbow parrotfish than in any other snorkeling spot in the area. As their name implies, rainbow parrotfish have as many colors as a rainbow and are among the largest of the parrot-fish group. They use their beaklike buckteeth to scrape the algae off rocks and coral, and in the process each individual fish may produce as much as a ton of sand in a year.

As you snorkel through Yal-Ku, you will notice changes in visibility and water temperature. This is the result of the blending of fresh and salt water. Fresh water seeps into the lagoon from underground springs. In one particular area next to the road's end, you will actually feel a current of fresh water, pushing you away from the edge. Visibility is about 15 feet and maximum depth is 10 feet. There are no rest rooms, refreshment stands, or shade at Yal-Ku.

AKUMAL

Km 255 (105 km south of Cancún)

Hundreds of years ago the Mayans discovered Akumal, which means the place of the turtle. In 1926, the Mason-Spinden expedition, sponsored by the *New York Times,* discovered Akumal again. In 1958, the CEDAM (Club of Explorations and Water Sports of Mexico) rediscovered Akumal while exploring the wreck of the Spanish galleon *El Matanzero.* On January 8, 1982, I discovered (for the first time ever) that people do not discover places, they simply discover that someone else already discovered them.

Tomorrow you, too, could discover Akumal, its golden sunshine, its tranquil bay, its spectacular underwater world, and its acrobatic coconut trees. Akumal has a popular yet uncrowded hotel on the beach, offering comfortable hotel rooms and family-sized bungalows, both reasonably priced.

Where to Stay

MODERATE

Hotel Villas Maya de Akumal *P.O. Box 984, Cancún, Q. Roo, Mexico.* Double rooms here are 2,000 pesos and have ceiling fans, hot and cold water, and mosaic floors. The hotel is right on the beach and has a swimming pool, restaurant, and bar. Tel. 30106.

DELUXE

Las Casitas, Akumal *P.O. Box 714, Cancún, Q. Roo, Mexico.* Las Casitas (the little houses) are beachfront bungalows with two bedrooms, two bathrooms, a sitting room, and a patio. Each casita is equipped with a refrigerator and ceiling fans and has full maid service. Each casita rents for 5,000 pesos a day with a maximum of five occupants.

Both accommodations are next to each other and share a central area with two restaurants, a bar, a snack bar, a craft shop, grocery store, and a dive shop. Tel. 31011 and 31068.

Restaurants

Restaurant Zasil There's no better restaurant south of Cancún than this one. Specialties include champagne lobster at 800 pesos, spring chicken *perigourdine* at 300 pesos, and New York steak for 600 pesos. Dinner 600 pesos. Open daily from 8:00 to 10:30 A.M., 1:30 to 4:00 P.M., and 7:30 to 10:00 P.M.

Restaurant Kalaan Serves set-menu lunch and dinner specials only. Dinner 600 pesos. Has same hours as Zasil restaurant.

Bar and Snack Bar Kalaan *On the beach.* Serves hamburgers 120 pesos, hot dogs 80 pesos, sandwiches 100 pesos, and other light lunch plates. Most domestic drinks cost 130 pesos.

Beaches and Activities

Akumal's beach is very shallow and calm. The reef, 150 yards offshore, breaks up the waves and currents, making the small Akumal Bay safe for swimming and snorkeling. The beach is shaded by a long, wide grove of oddly shaped coconut trees. As a result of the shallow sandy ground and occasional high winds, some of the coconut trees fall down. With their roots still attached to the ground, the trunks continue to grow at 90 degrees and other angles and in shapes that are unusual for a coconut tree. Compared to other beaches, the sand here is a bit hard. You may need more than your own natural padding to sit on it.

DEEP-SEA FISHING

As in the rest of this area, marlins, sailfish, dorado, bonito, etc. are the big-game species found here. Half-day outings cost between 2,800 and 3,600 pesos, depending on the type of fishing and the boat's size. Fishing arrangements should be made at the dive shop a couple of days before your outing.

SNORKELING

The best snorkeling in Akumal is in the reef area on the north side of the bay. The reef starts about 150 yards from the shore and is shallow enough so that you can wade most of the way into it.

Yal-Ku Lagoon is only two and a half miles north of Akumal. For access and description see Yal-Ku Lagoon. Mask, snorkel, and fins rent for 160 pesos at Akumal's dive shop.

SCUBA DIVING

The area around Akumal is a great one for diving. The sheer size of its reefs, the richness of its sea life, and the allure of its sunken ships rank it among the best diving spots in the Caribbean. But when it comes to shipwrecks, don't pack your diving gear and toothbrush expecting to find a treasure to pay for future diving trips. All of the area's sunken ships, like the Spanish galleon *El Matanzero*, sunk in 1741, have been corroded by the sea, or simply covered by tons of sand and coral. Occasionally divers (and even beachcombers) may find a few glass beads and other odd objects from *El Matanzero*. But the bulk of the salvage from this ship was rescued in 1959 and 1960 by the Club of Explorations and Water Sports of Mexico (CEDAM). Many of the objects brought out—cannons and belt buckles, for example—can be seen at CEDAM's tiny museum in Akumal.

Excursiones Akumal   *P.O. Box 984, Cancún.* 30 aluminum tanks,

Bauer 12 CFM compressor, motorboats, 775 pesos includes 2 tanks, 1,100 pesos for 3-hour resort course.

It would take years to explore the reefs in the Akumal area. Here are a few for starters.

Akumal Reef is located 150 yards offshore. This mile-and-a-half-wide reef serves as a natural protective barrier for Akumal's beach. Diving depths here are between 35 and 150 feet.

Yal-Ku Reef is located a mile and a half northeast of Akumal and is about 200 yards wide. Diving depths are between 45 and 80 feet.

Xak Reef, pronounced "Eeshak," is 3 miles north of Akumal. Its main features are 20- to 30-foot-high coral pillars.

Visibility in these reefs is approximately 90 feet. All are reef dives.

Coconut Bombs

I don't know how coconuts climb up to the top of coconut trees, but I know for a fact that ever since the law of gravity went into effect, they use it to crash down to the ground with the force of a crate of apples.

In a city, you don't cross a street before looking for oncoming traffic. In a coconut grove, you shouldn't walk, stand, camp, or park your car directly under the path of a bunch of coconuts.

Tours

ROBINSON CRUSOE CRUISES

Tours leave daily at 9:30 A.M. and require a minimum of 6 people. The tour is a combination of snorkeling, fishing, and diving, depending on the individual interests of the participants. The catch of fish and conch is prepared for lunch by the crew on a nearby beach. The price of the tour is 660 pesos per adult and includes a couple of cold drinks. A short glass-bottom boat tour is also available for 150 pesos per person.

THE RUINS

There are no organized tours of the ruins at Xelhá, Tulum, or Cobá in Akumal. However, you can organize your own by negotiating with one of the taxi drivers parked near the Akumal entrance gate. Reserve your taxi a day ahead of your trip.

A to Z

BANK

The closest bank is at Playa del Carmen, 36 km north of Akumal.

BUSES

You can catch buses north to Playa del Carmen and Cancún, and south to Xelhá and Tulum, on the main highway, a half mile from Akumal's entrance gate.

CAR RENTAL

VW Bugs and vans are for rent at Casita 305. The rates are a fraction higher than in Cancún.

GAS STATIONS

The gas stations at Puerto Morelos, 71 km north, and Tulum Ruins Junction, 24 km south, are the nearest ones to Akumal.

GROCERY STORE

The small grocery store near the entrance gate has a fair selection of unperishable foods, a few vegetables, soft drinks, and ice. Open 9:00 A.M. to 8:00 P.M.

MAIL

The reception desks at the hotels will mail your letters.

MUSEUM

The tiny Akumal Museum is located near the entrance gate and has an exhibit of coins, religious medals, cannons, tableware, bottles, and other items rescued from the sunken Spanish galleon *El Matanzero,* as well as a couple of pistols and brass objects from the HMS *Tweed,* which was sunk off the coast, about 1825. On the upper floor of the museum there is a collection of unmarked clay objects dug up from various Mayan sites. Admission is 10 pesos.

PLAYA AVENTURAS

Km 250 (110 km south of Cancún)

The entrance to this beach is marked by a sign that reads DIF. The beach is a quarter mile from the main road.

Playa Aventuras is a government children's hostel. Children from throughout the Yucatán Peninsula are brought here on government-paid vacations. Visitors should ask permission at the Administración for access to the beach and to the rest-room facilities.

The beach, which is very shallow and shaded by a dozen or so young coconut trees, is ideal for children. There is no food or drink for sale here and no camping allowed.

CHEMUYIL

Km 249 (111 km south of Cancún)

When they have had enough of rocking and rolling, when they are sick and tired of being seasick, when they grow old and tired, old waves retire to Chemuyil's peaceful bay. Here they loaf and play in the sun, and to keep themselves busy, they teach young fish to swim. Nothing disturbs their peace, but once in a while they get hot and reach for the shade of the coconut grove on the beach.

The camping fee on this government-operated beach is 66 pesos per person. The day visitor's fee is 22 pesos. The rest rooms and showers are very clean. There is a bar (open 10:00 A.M. to 5:00 P.M.) and picnic tables and benches.

Beaches and Activities

Chemuyil is a tiny horseshoe-shaped bay covering an area about twice the size of a football field. A reef stretching across the entrance of the bay breaks up the waves and currents and makes Chemuyil one of the safest beaches in the area. The beach is such an immaculate carpet of white sand that you will feel like wiping your feet before stepping on it. If a prize were given to the most beautiful coconut grove in the region, Chemuyil would win.

CAMPING

Vehicles cannot be driven onto the beach, but there is a large, shady parking lot about 50 yards from it.

Backpack campers are advised to camp on the south end of the beach, away from the influx of day visitors, which varies from a couple of dozen on weekdays to a hundred or more on weekends.

SNORKELING

The water is shallow and supercalm; the visibility is 30 to 40 feet, and like a parade of eager fashion models, beautifully dressed tropical fish are ready to display their colors and shapes before you.

The reef at the mouth of the bay is a good place to snorkel when the weather is good; otherwise, visibility is no more than 10 feet. Besides the standard reef fish, there are several schools of silvery mullet, a fish I did not see at other beaches in the region.

SHORE FISHING

You will need only to cast your baited hook 10 to 20 yards off the beach for jacks, white grunts, long-fin pompanos, bonefish, and occasionally a snapper. Spoons and plugs may also yield jacks and snappers. There is no bait available here, so bring your own.

XCACEL

Km 247 (113 km south of Cancún)

Xcacel (pronounced "Shacel") is an excellent beach for camping, snorkeling, fishing, and bird-watching. But even with these attractions Xcacel doesn't draw large crowds. At the end of December, at the height of the Christmas season, there were only 8 vehicles with 20 campers on this beach, which has the capacity to accommodate at least 40 vehicles.

Sea, sun, sand, and shade are included in the 66-peso-per-person camping fee. Xcacel has very clean rest rooms and showers, but does not have electricity, a restaurant, or any other camping facilities. For day visitors the fee is 22 pesos.

Beaches and Activities

Xcacel's beach is below a small, steep sand ridge right in front of the campgrounds. The beach grade is fairly steep and the waves are rather turbulent. The safest swimming area is a couple of hundred yards north of the campground. Here the waves are broken up by the reef in front of the beach. There is a slight current flowing south, 20 yards off the beach, but it is one that any fair swimmer can manage.

BIRD-WATCHING

An old dirt road runs parallel to the beach between Chemuyil, 2 kilometers north, and Xelhá, 2 kilometers south of Xcacel. Its ends can be found at the northeast and southeast corners of the campground.

Bordered by a thick grove of coconut trees and jungle vegetation, this road is a good place for early-morning bird-watching. As the sun filters through the frilled edges of coconut tree leaves, an amalgam of greens and yellows appears everywhere, and from every corner of the jungle, orioles, blackbirds, sparrows, finches, and other groups of feathery musicians compose their songs to the new day. Bad musicians that they are, bands of yellow-loreal parrots fly overhead disrupting the jungle's melodies with their screeching sounds.

BEACH HIKING/CAMPING

Hiking distance is 4 miles round trip on a mostly sandy beach, with some rocky obstacles. Attractions are beachcombing for coral and snorkeling in the Xelhá National Park (through the back door). Bring clothing for protection from the sun, head cover, snorkeling gear, footwear for rocky stretches, a bag to hold beachcombing finds, mosquito repellent (if camping), water, and food.

The hike between Xcacel and Xelhá, 2 miles to the south, can be done in one day or as a short 2- to 3-hour trip.

A couple of hundred yards from the start of your hike, you will get a close view of the wreck of the *Dublin Dan*. A silent proof of the fact that reefs are as dangerous as they are beautiful, this 40-foot boat is only one of the many shipwrecks that can be found in the reef areas of Mexico's Caribbean Sea. Past the *Dublin Dan* is the beginning of another small bay about the size of Xcacel Bay. Large sea-urchin shells, keyhole limpets, and small pieces of coral can be found around this point.

As opposed to Xcacel Bay's clear, turquoise water, the water in this bay is murky, full of seaweed and rocks. As you continue your hike, the beach is soft sand until you get to the south end of the bay. From there to the Xelhá Lagoon mouth the shoreline is solid rock.

Beachcombers, hold on to your eyes, because as you round the point you will discover a treasure chest of ivory-white coral from the size of marbles to the size of baseballs and footballs. You'll have a ball picking up the whitest and best polished pieces of dead coral to be found in the peninsula. Keep in mind that coral is as heavy as rocks and that it will add considerable weight to your baggage. From here to the mouth of the Xelhá Lagoon, it is only about a 10-minute walk.

Hermit Crabs

Don't be surprised to wake up in the morning and find what looks like bicycle-tire tracks around your tent left by hermit crabs as they forage around coconut groves.

Hermit crabs live in empty shells washed ashore by the waves. As a hermit crab grows, it simply moves into a larger shell.

Most of the hermit crabs found in Chemuyil and Xcacel live in 2- to 3-inch West Indian top shells. Quite a feat when you consider that the shell weighs about 15 times more than the crab itself.

SHORE FISHING

The best fishing spot is the sandy point (just before the rocky point) a couple of hundred yards north of the campground. Fish with bait in the coral-free white-water areas. One late afternoon, on my last visit here, I caught 3 1-pound blue runners, 3 mahogany snappers, and an immense and beautiful sunset.

SNORKELING

Xcacel's best snorkeling area is the reef located near the rocky point a couple of hundred yards north of the campground. The reef is about 150 yards long and its north end is connected to the rocky point.

XELHÁ NATIONAL PARK

Km 245 (115 km south of Cancún)

Xelhá is a natural aquarium carved out of the soft limestone terrain typical of most of the Yucatán Peninsula. The lagoon, with its many inlets and coves, covers an area of approximately 10 square acres. While snorkeling in its crystal waters, you will have to swim no more than a few yards to see several of the 50 or so species of colorful tropical fish that inhabit this little paradise. The entire lagoon is a fascinating labyrinth of underwater crevices, caves, and tunnels, each one hiding a treasure of multicolored fish. Unlike birds or other groups of wildlife, which flee at the sight of humans, the fish here are undisturbed and often curious when approached at a reasonable distance.

Angel, parrot, damsel, butterfly fish and many others will be quite indifferent to your presence until you are 5 or 6 feet away. Then they will swim away or hide between the rocks. They will poke their heads out from their hiding places to watch you. If you don't go away, they might disappear behind the rocks, go through their secret passages, and come out someplace else.

Swimming is prohibited in a few areas of the lagoon, and these are clearly marked with signs and buoys. The calm, clear waters average a depth of about 8 feet even at the edges. This is bad news for nonswimmers as there are no low spots to wade in.

Around the snorkeling area you will find clean, modern showers and rest rooms, rental lockers, a bar, and a restaurant with an ample seafood menu. Most main dishes cost 150 pesos. Snorkeling equipment rents for 70 pesos a day. Additionally, in the parking lot area you will find handcraft and beachwear shops, a small grocery store, and a cafeteria.

Tulum

Km 231 (129 km south of Cancún)

There is no sign marking the junction to the ruins of Tulum. Look instead for the El Crucero Motel sign; the ruins are three-quarters of a mile east. Buses drop off and pick up passengers at this point. Next to the Pemex gas station there are two good restaurants and a clean, comfortable hotel.

PUEBLO TULUM

Km 228 (132 km south of Cancún)

The tiny town of Tulum, not to be confused with Ruinas de Tulum, is on the main highway, 2 miles (3 kilometers) south of the junction to the ruins. It has three poorly stocked grocery stores and a vegetable and fruit store, no post or telegraph office, and not a single phone. The nearest long-distance phone office is in Playa del Carmen, 60 km north of here.

TULUM RUINS

Tulum Ruins are spectacularly set on a cliff, overlooking the Caribbean, and are the only excavated Mayan site located on the coast of the Yucatán Peninsula. It is a small site, compared to Chichén Itzá and Uxmal, that can be visited in an hour or less. Admission is 15 pesos, 10 on Sundays.

Tulum dates to about the sixth century A.D. The Mayan word *tulum* means wall, and it refers to the thick wall that was built around the city for protection from attacks. There are about 20 buildings of various sizes within Tulum's walled area. Three of the most interesting of them are described below.

The Temple of the Frescoes is located a few steps to your left from the entrance gate. The temple is a small, square building with a well-preserved fresco.

El Castillo ("the castle") is the largest building at Tulum, and is located on the edge of the cliff by the sea. A steep stairway leads to the top of the main structure and offers a good view of the ruins and the sea.

The Temple of the Descending God is a small temple located to the left of the castle. It is named after the figure of Ah Muzen Cab, the Mayan bee god. There are several other structures at Tulum, but none of them is of exceptional beauty or interest.

A slight current running south between the reef and the beach makes the snorkeling here a bit different from other places. I call it drift snorkeling; rather than snorkeling against the current, drift with it.

When I snorkel here, I walk to the area where the reef meets the rocky point. Once in the water I swim a few yards until I am in the current and simply drift with it, keeping an eye on the coral ahead of me so I can maneuver around it. I ride the current for a couple of hundred yards, before the reef ends and the waves start to get higher, and then get out of the water. I walk back to my starting point and repeat the tour.

Where to Stay

MODERATE

Motel El Crucero Double, 1,000 pesos. Ceiling fans, hot water, 16 rooms. Simple and clean. The only hotel at the ruins.

Restaurants

There are five restaurants at the parking area at the entrance to the ruins. All have very limited menus, with a few dishes of beef, pork, chicken, or fish for approximately 200 pesos. Breakfasts are approximately 100 pesos. They are open from 8:00 A.M. to about 5:00 P.M.

The two restaurants at the Tulum Ruins Junction offer a wider selection of dishes and a more appealing atmosphere. There is also a hotel there.

Restaurant El Faisan y El Venado Varied menu of Mexican and Yucatecán dishes. Most dishes cost about 200 pesos. Open 8:00 A.M. to 8:00 P.M. Clean and cool.

Restaurant El Crucero Offers a dozen or so main dishes in the 150- to 110-peso range. Also serves breakfasts. Good food.

FROM TULUM TO BOCA PAILA

The coastal road from the Tulum Ruins to Boca Paila starts at the southern end of the parking lot at the ruins. Boca Paila is 25 km (15 miles) south of Tulum. This road, however, goes as far as Punta Allen, 57 km (36 miles) south of Tulum Ruins. The road is paved for the first 6 kilometers; then it turns into an all-weather dirt road. It runs parallel to the coast and normally no more than a couple of hundred yards from it. Except for a few holes and bumps, this road is passable by all vehicles. Fill up your car with gas at the Tulum Ruins Junction.

There are no grocery stores between the Tulum Ruins and Punta Allen. The best place to stock up for your camping trip is Cancún. Playa del Carmen and Akumal's grocery stores are closer but they have a limited supply of foodstuffs.

Fresh water is in short supply south of the Tulum Ruins. The only source of fresh water here is from shallow wells which produce a meager supply of slightly salty water.

Places to stay south of Tulum Ruins include La Villa de Boca Paila (moderate); Cabañas Tulum (budget); two rustic paying campgrounds (The Reef and "No Name"); several free beach camping spots, and a couple of "hip slums."

"Hip slums," as I define them, are any beach accommodations (campgrounds, cabañas, *palapas*, etc.) with slumlike sanitary and living conditions, patronized mostly by American, Canadian, and European travelers on tight budgets.

───────── *Where to Stay* ─────────

El Mirador *Km 0.5*, campground and cabañas. When you first arrive at El Mirador you think you have walked into a Mayan jungle village. Then you start looking for the dark-skinned, dark-haired

Mayan natives, and as you look into the *palapa* huts you discover instead blond, blue-eyed foreigners gone native. Living is simple here. You sleep in your own hammock, cook in fire pits, take bucket showers, and read by candlelight. Were it not for the inadequate sanitary conditions, El Mirador would be a simple but very inviting campground.

Camping is 15 pesos per person, cabaña space is 30 pesos per person.

Camping El Paraíso *Km 1,* campgrounds and cabañas. El Paraíso ("the Paradise") is a ridiculous name for a place with dumpy grounds, filthy rest rooms, and no showers. To make things worse, in a region where every campground is a beautiful grove of coconut trees, El Paraíso does not even offer the shade of a blade of grass.

The Reef Campground *Km 7.* El Arrecife ("the Reef") is only 4 miles from the crowded campgrounds by the ruins, and it is a different world. It is virtually empty most of the time and it has clean grounds, rest rooms, and no water-supply problem. There is one well for clothes washing and showers and one for drinking water (but boil your water anyway).

The camping rate is 25 pesos per person.

Cabañas Tulum *Km 8.* This budget hotel has clean, simple beachfront rooms with asbestos roofs, individual bathrooms with cold water—and silly me forgot whether they have ceiling fans. Rooms cost 500 pesos for one to three occupants.

The Cabañas restaurant is the only budget restaurant south of the ruins with simple, inexpensive, and good food, prepared and served in clean, pleasant surroundings. Lunch and dinner dishes cost approximately 100 pesos.

"Twenty-five Pesos" Campground *Km 12.* When I arrived at this clean, empty campground, I asked the elderly Mayan groundskeeper, "How much does it cost to camp here?" He answered with a smile and a heavy Mayan accent, "Twentee-five pesos." I then asked, "What is the name of the campground?"; he replied, "Twenty-five pesos." I started to suspect that was the only expression he knew, and to check my theory, I asked him, "Are mosquitoes expensive around here?" Naturally his answer was "Twenty-five pesos." Actually mosquitoes are included in the camping rate, and to keep them at a distance, set your tent on or beyond the sand ridge by the beach. There are no toilets and no showers here. There is a well with sufficient water for about 15 campers. At Christmas, though, with 30 or more people camping here, the water supply is inadequate.

Boca Paila Bridge

Km 25 (Tulum Ruins to Punta Allen Road)

The Boca Paila Bridge is at the canal that connects the Boca Paila lagoons with the Caribbean Sea. The bridge is a wooden structure built about ten years ago. At first it looks as if it might collapse with the weight of a vehicle, but it is solidly built and cars and trucks cross it all the time. The area of the bridge is a good one for camping and one of the best in the peninsula for fishing and bird-watching. La Villa de Boca Paila is the only hotel here, and there is not as much as a single refreshment stand. Come prepared with all the food and water that you will need.

Where to Stay

MODERATE

Pez Maya Fishing Resort *Km 25, at the Boca Paila Bridge.* Pez Maya specializes in lagoon fishing and accepts guests by reservation only. Write to: Pez Maya; P.O. Box 9; Cozumel, Q. Roo, Mexico.

DELUXE

La Villa de Boca Paila *Km 15, Ruinas Tulum–Punta Allen Road.* Double, 3,000 pesos, includes breakfast and lunch. Has 8 large, round cabañas each with 2 bedrooms, 2 bathrooms, kitchenette, and living room. For reservations, write: La Villa de Boca Paila; P.O. Box 159; Mérida, Yucatán, Mexico.

The Beach

The beach north and south of the lagoon's mouth is a wide, desolate vastness of sand, edged by thick jungle vegetation and coconut trees. It's the kind of beach where, if you wish, you could disappear from civilization and not see a soul for weeks.

The waves are about a foot high in good weather. The milky turquoise water here is not clear enough for diving and snorkeling.

CAMPING

Take the road to the beach at the north end of the bridge. Drive about 300 yards to the grassy area between the lagoon and the beach. There is no shade here. But the breeze is fresh and keeps away the lagoon's abundant mosquito population. However, make sure you have mosquito repellent with you, just in case the breeze dies down. Bury all your refuse, as there are no cleaning crews around here.

BIRD-WATCHING

The huge lagoons of the Boca Paila region are the home of many water-bird species. On a single morning of bird-watching, I saw sandwich and royal terns, mangrove swallows, magnificent frigate birds, brown pelicans, olivaceous cormorants, one pinnated bittern, and one ruddy crake.

SHORE FISHING

Sports fishermen from the United States and Canada fly especially to Boca Paila to fish in its lagoons for tarpon, permit snook, and bonefish. This type of fishing requires special tackle and skills, but with a hook and a hand line you should be able to land grunts, snappers, jacks, and other fresh fish for your frying pan.

There are two good fishing spots. On the bridge, fish with cut bait and check it frequently as sergeant majors and other freeloaders will eat it off the hook. At the mouth of the lagoon, where all fish leaving and entering the lagoon pass through, a little fishing experience and a little luck could produce some surprising catches.

Cobá

──────────── *Getting There* ────────────

Car There are two access routes to Cobá. From Mérida, take Highway 180 toward Cancún as far as Nuevo Xcan, 230 km (143 miles) away. The Cobá highway is at Nuevo Xcan's main plaza. It's 45 km (28 miles) to Cobá from here.

From Cancún, take the highway to the Tulum Ruins Junction, 131 km (81 miles) south. Two kilometers south of this junction is the Cobá highway. It's 45 km (26 miles) to Cobá from the main highway.

Bus Mérida and Cancún are the best places to leave from.

──────────── *The Ruins of Cobá* ────────────

There is almost no archaeological literature available on Cobá. The following is a brief description of the site, with information on how to get to the different ruin groupings.

It's a long way from one group of ruins to another, so you should come prepared with good walking shoes and a water canteen for the heat of the day. Don't think of Cobá solely as ruins. The jungle around it is full of a fascinating variety of wildlife. Birds and lizards, for example, are abundant. Admission: 5 pesos.

A few yards from the entrance, to your right, is the tall pyramid called **the Church.** It is 105 steep steps to the top, but the view of the lagoons and the jungle, with its towering *ramones* trees, is well worth the climb.

Las Pinturas is a half mile east of the Church on the main path. This group of ruins is named after the painting on the top of the small pyramid there. A palm-leaf awning has been placed over this well-preserved painting to protect it from the sun's rays. At the base of the pyramid are the remnants of a building with round pillars. Return to the main path and follow the signs to Conjunto Macanxoc.

Conjunto Macanxoc is about a mile away from Las Pinturas, through a tunnel of lush, green vegetation. Macanxoc is a group of eight magnificent stelae. The first stela is 10 feet high, with a carving of a man with a headdress. Just behind it is a larger one, set as if on an altar. The carvings on this stela are very clear and show two figures, one crouching and one kneeling. To the left of this stela are six others, all set in mysterious little corners of the jungle. Return past Las Pinturas to the sign for Nohoch Mul.

From the main path it's about a mile to **Nohoch Mul.** As you arrive at this group of ruins you'll see a building with a stela in front of it. To the left is the great pyramid of Nohoch Mul. There are 120 steps to the top of the pyramid, which is the second tallest in the peninsula, after the pyramid of Kinich Kamo, located at Izamal, Yucatán State.

Where to Stay

Ask around town for rooms and places to hang your hammock, but come prepared with mosquito netting or repellent.

MODERATE

Villa Arqueológica Hotel   Double, 1,600 pesos. Ceiling fans, hot water, swimming pool, and bar. The restaurant here is first class and offers good dinners for under 600 pesos. For peace, quiet, and service, this hotel is worth the special trip from any point in the Yucatán Peninsula.

Restaurants

Restaurant Isabel offers an inexpensive lunch of *pollo à la Mexicana,* grilled pork, and beef dishes for 200 pesos. Superb service and good food.

APPENDIX

Food Guide

As many well-seasoned travelers know, all Mexican cooking is not spicy and does not consist solely of enchiladas and tacos. There are innumerable local, regional, and national dishes found in every corner of the country. In order to make it easier to discover these, here is a guide to help you "digest" the language found on menus.

Achiote   A mild spice typical of the Yucatán Peninsula, which is used in many of its delicious dishes such as *cochinita pibil* and pork or chicken à la Yucateca. It's also used in *Tik-In-Chik*, barbecued fish. *Achiote* paste can be bought in grocery stores and will add some spice to anything fried, baked, or barbecued.

Adobo   A sauce made with *chile ancho*, one of the mildest of dry chiles. Other ingredients are tomatoes, garlic, onion, white pepper, cumin, cloves, oregano, and cinnamon. *Adobo* is usually added to pork dishes, but it can also be used with beef or chicken. If you would like a spicy dish that won't kill all your taste buds, try *adobo*.

Antojitos   The word literally means "a little craving" and refers to a specific category of foods that includes tacos, enchiladas, tostadas, and *quesadillas*.

──────────── **BEBIDAS (BEVERAGES)** ────────────

Café negro	black coffee
Café con crema	coffee with cream
Café con leche	coffee with milk
Té de manzanilla	camomile tea
Té de yerba buena	mint tea
Té negro	black tea
Té helado	iced tea
Té de azar	orange-blossom tea
Refresco	soft drink

Aguas de Frutas   Fruit drinks are very common in Mexico. They are sold at street stands and restaurants throughout the Yucatán Peninsula.

Agua de limón	lemonade
Agua de Jamaica	hibiscus-flower water
Agua de horchata	rice water
Agua de tamarindo	tamarind water
Naranjada	orangeade

Cerveza (beer)   *Montejo*, *XXX (Tres Equis)*, *Modelo*, *Corona*, *Superior*, and *Carta Blanca* are light beers. *Leon Negra* is a dark beer.

Jugos y Licuados   Juices and fruit drinks are sold throughout Mexico at street stands or formal juice bars with rows, piles, and pyramids of papayas, oranges, pineapple, watermelons, and so on.

Licuados are made in a blender *(licuadora)* with fresh fruit slices, purified or filtered water or milk, and sugar.

Vino   There are many brands of Mexican wine as well as imported wines available throughout the Yucatán.

Vino tinto	red wine
Vino blanco	white wine
Vino rosado	rosé wine
Champaña	champagne
Sidra or *champaña*	apple cider

Chiles rellenos   Many people are acquainted with these stuffed peppers. North of the border, *chiles rellenos* are made with bell peppers; in Mexico, they are made with the mildly *picante* ("hot") *chile poblano*. Cheese or ground meat is the most common stuffing, but tuna fish or sardines are often used.

─────────────── **ENSALADAS (SALADS)** ───────────────

Many visitors avoid salads for fear of catching *turista* or other stomach disorders as a result of the water in which the vegetables are washed. Personally, when a salad is served with the main dish, I ask to have it brought to me on a separate plate. I then drain the liquid from the salad and squeeze the juice of a lime onto it. In Mexico, we believe that lime kills the bacteria in the salad. While eating the rest of the meal, I occasionally stir the salad, eating it at the end of the meal in order to allow time for the lime to work.

The most common vegetables used in salads are *lechuga* (lettuce), *col* (cabbage), *jitomate* (tomato), *pepino* (cucumber), *cebolla* (onion), and *pimiento verde* (green pepper).

Mealtimes

Desayuno (**breakfast**) *Café con leche,* which is milk with instant coffee or milk with coffee concentrate, and *pan dulce* (sweet rolls) is the most common breakfast throughout Mexico.

However, eggs in various styles or meat or pancakes are also standard breakfast foods.

Comida (**lunch**) Just like the sun, Mexican appetite is at its zenith during this part of the day. Ironically, though, while the sun is burning up a few calories, Mexicans are storing them up for use in the cooler parts of the day. *Comida,* the Mexican's main meal, is served somewhere between 2:00 and 4:00 P.M., except on workdays when it is served about 1:00 P.M.

Cena (**supper or dinner**) *Cena* can be a full-course meal, like dinner in North America, or a light meal of *café con leche* and *pan dulce.* Usually, Mexicans have *cena* after 8:00 P.M.

FRUTAS (FRUITS)

Mexico is fresh fruit country and although the Yucatán Peninsula does not produce much fruit, truckloads arrive here daily from Campeche, Tabasco, Chiapas, Veracruz, and other fruit-producing states of Mexico.

limón	lemon	*guayaba*	guava
lima	lime	*guanábana*	guanabana
naranja	orange	*granada*	pomegranate
toronja	grapefruit	*tamarind*	tamarind
melón	cantaloupe	*chabacano*	apricot
sandía	watermelon	*durazno*	peach
papaya	papaya	*zapote blanco*	white zapote
mango	mango	*zapote negro*	black zapote
mamey	mamey	*uva*	grape
plátano	banana	*pasa*	raisin
piña	pineapple	*uva pasa*	prune
fresa	strawberry	*ciruela*	plum
coco	coconut		

HUEVOS (EGGS)

Huevos (pronounced "waybose") are cooked in a variety of styles in Mexico. Breakfast *(desayuno)* dishes are often served with a portion of refried beans and tortillas or bread.

Huevos tibios	three-minute eggs
Huevos revueltos	scrambled eggs
Huevos con jamón	ham and eggs
Huevos con chorizo	sausage and eggs
Huevos con frijoles	refried beans and eggs
Huevos cocidos (duros)	hard-boiled eggs
Omelet de jamón	ham omelet
Omelet de hongos	mushroom omelet
Omelet de queso	cheese omelet
Omelet surtido	mixed omelet
Huevos fritos	sunny-side-up eggs

Huevos à la Mexicana Two eggs scrambled with chopped tomatoes, onion, and *serrano*.

Huevos rancheros Two fried eggs served on a lightly fried tortilla topped with tomato sauce.

Huevos Motuleños Motul-style eggs are a Yucatecán invention consisting of a fried tortilla, fried eggs, tomato sauce, ham, shredded cheese, and peas.

How Is It?

Bueno, muy bueno: Good, very good
Delicioso: Delicious
Sabroso, muy sabroso: Tasty, very tasty
Rico, muy rico: Also means tasty or very tasty
Picante, muy picante: Spicy hot, very hot
Picoso: Same as picante
Pica poco: A bit picante
Pica mucho: Very picante
No pica: It's not picante
Picante pero sabroso: Picante but tasty
Para chuparse los dedos: Finger-licking good

—————————— MARISCOS (SEAFOOD) ——————————

Seafood restaurants abound in the coastal towns and cities of the Yucatán Peninsula. Once you go into the interior, however, seafood is very scarce except in Mérida.

Caracol (conch) and *tortuga* (turtle) are considered endangered species by some concerned Mexicans, and therefore dishes made with the meat of these animals are not included.

Camarones	shrimp
Ceviche de camarón	shrimp ceviche
Camarón empanizado	breaded shrimp
Camarón natural	boiled shrimp
Brocheta de camarón	shrimp brochette
Camarón à la parrilla	grilled shrimp
Camarón al mojo de ajo	garlic-fried shrimp
Camarón à la gabardina	breaded shrimp
Langosta al natural	boiled lobster
Langosta al mojo de ajo	garlic-fried lobster
Langosta à la parrilla	grilled lobster
Langosta empanizada	breaded lobster
Langosta revuelta en huevo	lobster dipped in egg batter
Filete de pescado à la Milaneza	breaded fish fillet
Filete de pescado al mojo de ajo	garlic-fried fish fillet
Filete de pescado à la parrilla	grilled fish fillet

Ceviche A very popular seafood dish, made with boned fillets of red snapper cut into small chunks. The raw fish is then marinated for a couple of hours in enough lime juice to cover it. Black pepper, thyme, rosemary, and salt are added to the fish as it marinates. The acid in the lime juice "cooks" the fish, and at the end of 2 hours, it's ready. Serve with crackers or fried tortilla chips. This is the commercial recipe. A good homemade ceviche should also have chopped tomatoes, onions, parsley, garlic, and avocado. Then it's really mmmm! Ceviche can also be made with cooked shrimp, squid *(calamar)*, and octopus *(pulpo)*.

Cocteles Seafood cocktails are made with raw oysters, cooked shrimp, octopus, lobster, or squid, and are served with cocktail sauce, lime juice, and usually a touch of hot sauce.

Langosta Lobsters found in the Caribbean Sea are spiny ones without claws.

Pescado frito Whole fried fish is one of the most popular seafood dishes. It's usually made with pan-sized fish such as grunts and small snappers, and served with a mixed salad, cabbage, or french fries.

Filete de pescado The best fish fillets are from red snapper *(huachinango)* or grouper *(cabrilla)*, but many other fish, including young shark *(cazón)*, are also used.

Filete à la Veracruzana This dish originated in the state of Veracruz and is one of Mexico's favorites. It consists of red snapper *(huachinango)* fillets cooked with chopped tomatoes, onion, garlic, olives, olive oil, and fragrant spices.

MOLES

Mole Poblano Originally from Puebla State in central Mexico, *mole* is the traditional dish for birthday parties and weddings. It's an elaborate dish containing some twenty different ingredients such as chocolate, sesame seeds, raisins, fried and ground bread and tortillas, four different kinds of dried chiles, garlic, onions, and much more. All the ingredients are ground into a sauce, which is served over chicken or turkey.

Mole rojo or *chile rojo* A simple, quick red *mole* made with chiles *(ancho* and *cascabel)*, tomatoes, garlic, and any meat. This dish can turn you into a flamethrower.

Mole verde or *chile verde* Green tomatoes *(tomates)*, used in this dish, are a common ingredient in Mexican cooking. They are smaller than a regular tomato *(jitomate)*, but when ripe they turn yellow green instead of red. Green tomatoes are never eaten raw, as they are quite acid. Besides green tomatoes, *mole verde* is made with fresh *chile serrano*, garlic, onion, and cilantro (a type of parsley). Pork, beef, or chicken is used in this dish. It is another "highly flammable" dish.

PAVO (TURKEY)

Pavo en relleno blanco The white stuffing of this baked-turkey dish consists of ground pork mixed with olives, capers, raisins, and almonds; a delicious Yucatecán specialty.

Pavo en relleno negro The stuffing of this slightly piquant baked-turkey dish is made with ground pork, toasted *chile negro*, tomato, *achiote*, pepper, lard, and vinegar.

POLLO (CHICKEN)

Pollo frito Fried chicken.

Pollo con arroz Chicken with rice, also called *arroz con pollo*.

Pollo rostizado Roasted chicken, also called *pollo al pastor* (shepherd chicken).

Pollo à las brasas Coal-roasted chicken.

Pollo pibil Chicken pieces basted with *achiote*, wrapped in banana leaves with chopped tomato, onion, and *epazote*, and baked.

Pollo Ticuleño Chicken pieces basted with a mixture of lime, salt, and pepper, breaded and fried; served in tomato sauce.

Pollo à la Yucateca *Pollo* basted with a paste of *achiote*, salt, pepper, and lime, and then fried.

POSTRES (DESSERTS)

Flan Custard is the most popular Mexican dessert.

Arroz con leche Rice cooked in milk with raisins, cinnamon, and vanilla.

Nieve *Nieve* means both "ice cream" and "snow" in Spanish, but in sunny Mexico there is little chance you'll ever be served strawberry snow. Sherbet is called *nieve de agua*, while ice cream is called *nieve de leche*. The most popular ice cream flavors are *coco*, *chocolate*, *nuez* (walnut), *piñon* (pine nut), *vainilla*, *café*, and *pistache*.

Pay The spelling of the English word "pie" happens to mean "foot" in Spanish. Since no one in Mexico would have a foot for dessert, the spelling of the word became p-a-y, pronounced just like pie.

Pastel Cake comes in many shapes and flavors, and with a variety of icings.

Plátano frito Fried bananas are slices of *plátano macho* (plantain) fried or baked, and topped with sour cream. If they are fried in butter they are even better.

PUERCO (PORK)

Pork is used in some typical Yucatecán dishes such as *cochinita pibil* and *puerco à la Yucateca*.

Chuletas de puerco	fried pork chops
Chuleta Milaneza	breaded pork chop

Cochinita pibil Pork basted with *achiote*, salt, and spices, wrapped in banana leaves and baked. A great Yucatecán dish!

Is It Chili Down South?

When it's chilly up north, it's "chili" down south, and just like Eskimos have two dozen or so names for different types of snow and ice, Mexicans have at least that many different types of chiles.

To begin with, the Mexican name of this high explosive is *chile* (pronounced "cheeleh"), and the Spanish words used to describe its potency are *picante* or *picoso*. They translate literally into English as "stingy" or "prickly." The English word "hot" translates into Spanish as *caliente* and is used only to indicate temperature.

Many Mexican dishes are traditionally made with one or more types of chiles, and without them, they would be something entirely different. *Mole poblano,* for example, is one such dish. Many other dishes can be made with or without chile. In tourist areas, such as Cancún, restaurants often modify their *picante* plates to suit the palates of foreign visitors. To be on the safe side, however, always ask how *picante* a particular dish is.

In the Yucatán Peninsula, watch out for any dish containing *chile habanero*. It's a dynamite stick in disguise.

Pierna de puerco à la Yucateca   Pork-leg slices basted with *achiote* and vinegar, fried with onion slices.

Pierna de puerco   Baked pork leg cut in slices and served with a sauce or in tortas.

Poc-chuc   Pork-leg roast served with a tomato and chile sauce, fried onion, parsley, and sour orange. Another typical Yucatecán dish.

--- RES (BEEF) ---

Albóndigas   Meatballs are cooked in many stocks and sauces. The most common are *albóndigas en jitomate* (meatballs in tomato sauce) and *albóndigas al chipotle* (meatballs in *chipotle chile* and tomato sauce).

Biftec   Some restaurants in the larger cities specialize in American steak cuts such as T-bone *(tibón)* and sirloin *(sirlón)*. Mexican steaks have the thickness of a shoe sole, and at times, its consistency. The better the restaurant, the more tender the steak.

Biftec frito   Pan-fried steak is also known as *carne asada*.

Filete de res   A better quality, more tender steak.

Filete de res Tampiqueña   Tampico-style fillet is a pan-fried steak served with an enchilada, refried beans, and rice.

Filete de res à la Mexicana   Steak cooked in tomato sauce with garlic and onions.

Picadillo   Ground beef served with tomatoes, onions, garlic, and spices; diced zucchini is sometimes added.

———————— SOPAS (SOUPS) ————————

A Mexican meal always starts with soup. Broths *(caldos)*, consommés, rice *(arroz)*, and pasta are considered soups and first courses and are therefore always served at the beginning of full-course meals.

Caldo de pollo	chicken broth
Consomé de pollo	chicken consommé
Consomé de res	beef consommé
Consomé de camarón	shrimp consommé
Sopa de lentejas	lentil soup
Sopa Juliana or *de verduras*	vegetable soup

Sopa de ajo   Fried garlic and bread chunks cooked in chicken broth; a good *sopa de ajo* should also have *chorizo* (sausage).

Sopa de arroz   The rice may be cooked in tomato sauce, similar to what is called Spanish rice in the United States. Without tomato sauce, it's called *sopa de arroz al natural*.

Sopa de lima   This typical Yucatecán soup is made with chicken broth, tomato, onion, Mexican parsley *(cilantro)*, chicken chunks, fried tortilla chips, and lime juice; sometimes it's served with lime slices in it.

Sopa de pasta   There are about two dozen shapes of pasta used for soups; some of the most common are *fideo* (vermicelli), *tallarín* (pasta-shaped egg noodles), *letras* (alphabet soup), and *codo* (elbow macaroni). The most common way to make pasta soup is to cook the pasta lightly, add tomato sauce with garlic and onion, and chicken consommé.

Sopa de pescado   There are many recipes for fish soup, but it is most often made with tomato sauce, potatoes, carrots, and spices such as thyme and rosemary.

Sopa tártara Similar to chicken consommé, but as the boiling consommé is served in the bowl a raw egg is cracked into it.

TAMALES

In Mexico, real tamales are made with rough ground-corn dough with pork lard *(manteca)* and wrapped in corn husks (central Mexico) or banana leaves (coastal areas of Mexico and the Yucatán Peninsula). Pork or chicken or raisins and cinnamon are also added to tamales before they are steam-cooked for a couple of hours. If your tamales are not served on corn husks or banana leaves, you could very well sue the restaurant for ta-mal practice. The singular of *tamales* is *tamal,* and not *tamale.*

TORTAS

Tortas are the Mexican cousins of sandwiches. They are made with small bread loaves about the size of a fist, and like sandwiches, they have just about any filler. Sour cream, onion and tomato slices, avocado *(aguacate),* and a couple of slices of *chile jalapeño* are the usual fixings of tortas.

TORTILLAS

Tortillas are made from a dough of boiled ground corn, shaped like a thin pancake, and cooked on a hot iron skillet. Tortillas made with wheat flour are called *tortillas de harina,* but they are not common in the Yucatán Peninsula. Flour-tortilla tacos are called burritos.

Tortillas change their name when they are combined with other foods, just as a piece of bread becomes a sandwich when you put ham, mayonnaise, and other goodies on it. Here are some of the most common dishes that use tortillas as a base.

Chilaquiles Made with crumbled, dried tortillas, lightly browned in oil. Tomato, garlic, onion, and *chile serrano* sauce are then added. The sauce is cooked on a low flame until the liquid evaporates and then served with shredded cheese and sour cream.

Enchiladas Made with a lightly fried tortilla, which is dipped into a red or green chile sauce and filled with meat or chicken. The enchilada is then folded or rolled and usually topped with cheese and sour cream.

Flautas Rolled, deep-fried tortillas filled with shredded meat; their shape resembles a flute, therefore the Spanish name. *Flautas* are topped with sour cream and shredded cheese.

Quesadillas The word *quesadilla* comes from the combination of the words *queso* (cheese) and tortilla. The best *quesadillas* are made by melting Oaxaca cheese and an herb called *epazote*.

Sopa de tortilla A very good soup, especially the day after it is made. It's made like *chilaquiles,* except that chicken consommé and *epizote* are added to the fried tomato, garlic, and onion sauce.

Tacos Take a tortilla, put a couple of spoonfuls of any food in it, fold it, and presto! You have a taco.

Tostadas Crisp, fried tortillas, with layers of refried beans, shredded pork, beef or chicken, lettuce, tomato slices, avocado, and sour cream. It's easy to know when you are eating a tostada because it always crumbles to pieces on the first bite. *Salbutes* and *panuchos* are Yucatecán versions of tostadas.

First Aid

Turista   What is it?

Bacteria are really the major culprit in *turista* or "Montezuma's revenge." Bacteria, particularly one type, *e. coli,* are a normal part of any person's digestive tract, no matter where in the world he or she resides. However, some enteric or intestinal bacteria differ slightly from others. These different bacteria enjoy the digestive · tracts of people new to their particular region; and the worst of these toxic bacteria often live in tropical zones.

The major reason most people get *turista* or diarrhea is because their systems have not had time to adjust to the new bacteria. When your body initially fights new bacteria, it needs plenty of fluids, i.e., water. Too much heat, alcohol, and sunburn can cause dehydration and a breakdown of the body's built-in defenses. This results in *turista,* which in turn results in further fluid loss. This loss further weakens the body's resistance to illness, and so a cycle is formed. The trick, of course, is to prevent this cycle from starting in the first place. To avoid getting *turista,* follow this advice:

1. During your visit, stick to bottled drinks, distilled and boiled water. *Never drink tap water!*

2. Don't drink alcoholic beverages in excess; they dehydrate you.

3. Do not spend too much time out in the sun; this too will dehydrate you.

4. Take a *siesta,* or relax in the shade during the hottest part of the day (usually between noon and three in the afternoon).

5. Take acidophilus tablets at least 5 days before you arrive in Mexico and continue taking them throughout your stay.

If you do become ill, *turista* will usually manifest itself in the form of diarrhea, but in some cases it will also be accompanied by nausea and/or vomiting.

For diarrhea, mash a couple of fairly green bananas mixed with a couple of tablespoons of Donnamycina P.G. This medicine is available over the counter in just about every *farmacia* in Mexico. Donnamycina P.G. will cut down the colony count of the *e. coli* bacteria in your afflicted intestinal tract and will allow your natural immune system to adapt to the new bacteria (toxic *coli*).

If you are nauseous and vomiting, take Tigon in capsule form *(cap-soulas)*; one every 6 to 8 hours should help. If this or Alka-Seltzer doesn't work, and if the nausea lasts more than 24 hours, a doctor or clinic should be sought.

Too Much Sun With mild sunburn there is redness and the skin feels hot to the touch, but no fever, nausea, vomiting, or blistering.

One folk remedy is to soak the sunburned areas with vinegar or olive oil; let it stay on for a half hour, then rinse off. Aside from smelling like a tossed green salad, the mild sunburn will quickly become a tan.

For moderate and severe sunburn, there are a number of medications available over the counter in pharmacies in Mexico. Solarcaine is by far the most popular remedy (in combination with aloe-vera cream). Relief is immediate due to the benzocaine that this preparation contains.

Another folk remedy for moderate sunburn is lime juice, followed by a paste made with equal amounts of papaya and well-mashed papaya seeds. Now you will feel like a fruit salad, but the *papaína* from the papaya seeds, which is used in commercial meat tenderizers, may give you relief. After an hour or so, wash off the papaya paste and apply a moisturizing cream, such as *crema de pepinos*. Most important, remember to stay out of the sun, drink plenty of liquids, and wear a hat.

For the severest burns, apply Neosporin unguentine, a three-way antibiotic salve. A light coat of this cream, plenty of shade, and liquids will usually do the trick.

Sea-Urchin Spines First remove the spine slowly and carefully with pointed tweezers and/or a sharp sturdy needle; then get the puncture to bleed. Next, apply cortisone cream over the afflicted area every 8 to 12 hours. It is a good general preparation for scrapes and cuts in a tropical area such as the Yucatán.

Coral Scratches First wash off the afflicted area with warm salt water; then apply cortisone cream. The pain will go away in a short while.

Jellyfish Stings Wash the afflicted area with warm salt water, then apply a mixture of Benadryl *(jarabe)* and cortisone cream. Cold compresses also help relieve the swelling and redness.

A common folk remedy is to wash the afflicted area with warm salt water and then apply a paste of papaya seeds. Leave it on for one hour; then wash it off. Repeat the treatment if the stinging persists.

Scorpion Stings Scorpion stings are very seldom a problem to visitors in the Yucatán Peninsula. In general, the severity of a scorpion sting depends on the size and species of scorpion, the size of the person stung, and the degree of his or her allergic reaction to the sting. The species of scorpions found in the Yucatán Peninsula, however, are not considered particularly dangerous.

Just to be safe, the following precautions are advisable, especially for campers.

Scorpions are nocturnal creatures. They like dry, woody areas. They love to hide in cracks, gaps, under tents, inside shoes, etc. So don't walk barefoot in the darkness around *palapa* or wood buildings or dry brush, and shine a flashlight before reaching into dark places.

If stung by a scorpion, stay calm. To inhibit the spread of the poison, apply ice to the affected area and take an antihistamine. If symptoms such as pain, numbness, difficulty in breathing, and stiffness of the jaw persist or seem severe, then seek medical attention as soon as possible.

Useful Spanish Expressions

In the Bank *En el Banco*

I wish to change ____ .
Deseo cambiar ____ .

  American dollars
  Dólares Americanos

  Canadian dollars
  Dólares Canadienses

  Dollar bills
  Dólares en billetes

  Traveler's checks
  Cheques de viajero

Do you charge a commission?
¿Cobran una comisión?

What is the commission you charge?
¿De cuánto es la comisión que cobran?

What is the exchange rate?
¿Cuál es la taza de cambio?

Exchange
Cambios

Exchange hours
Horas de cambio

When are the exchange hours?
¿Cuáles son las horas de cambio?

Where is another bank?
¿Dónde hay otro banco?

On the Beach *En la Playa*

The sand
La arena

The water
El agua

The wave
La ola

The sun
El sol

The coconut
El coco

The coconut tree
El cocotero, la palmera

The shell
La concha

It's very hot.
Hace mucho calor.

The tide
La marea

Gee, it's hot!
¡Qué calor!

High tide
Marea alta

It's cloudy.
Está nublado.

Low tide
Marea baja

Is it going to rain?
¿Va a llover?

Is there a current?
¿Hay corriente?

It's raining.
Está lloviendo.

Is there an undertow?
¿Hay resaca?

Wind
El viento

Heat
Calor

It's windy.
Hace viento.

It's hot.
Hace calor.

──────────────── **On the Bus** *En el Camión* ────────────────

Bus
Autobús or *camión*

When are there buses for ___ ?
¿A que hora hay camiones a ___ ?

Direct
Directo

How much is the fare to ___ ?
¿Cuánto cuesta el pasaje a ___ ?

The driver
El chofer

Is there a toilet on the bus?
¿Hay baño en el camión?

Does the bus go by ___ ?
¿Pasa por ___ el autobús?

I'd like a ticket for ___ at ___ (time).
Quiero un boleto para ___ a las ___ .

I'd like a seat by the window.
Quisiera un asiento junto a la ventanilla.

USEFUL SPANISH EXPRESSIONS

Directions *Direcciones*

To the right
A la derecha

To the left
A la izquierda

Straight ahead
Derecho

One block from here
A una cuadra de aquí

On the corner
En la esquina

In front
En frente

Near
Cerca

Far
Lejos

On the Ferry *En el Ferry*

Passenger boat
Lancha de pasajeros

The pier
El embarcadero

What time does the next boat for ____ leave?
¿A qué hora sale la próxima lancha a ____ ?

How long does it take from ____ to ____ ?
¿Cuánto tiempo toma de ____ a ____ ?

How much is the fare to ____ ?
¿Cuánto cuesta el pasaje a ____ ?

Is there a toilet on the boat?
¿Hay un baño en la lancha?

Greetings and Farewells *Saludos y Despedidas*

Hi
Hola

How goes it?
¿Qué tal?

How are you?
¿Cómo está? (singular)
¿Cómo están? (plural)

Good morning
Buenos días

Good afternoon
Buenas tardes

Good night
Buenas noches

Until tomorrow
Hasta mañana

See you, so long
Hasta luego

On the Highway *En la Carretera*

Paved road
Camino pavimentado

Dirt road
Camino de terracería

Hole
Bache

Curve
Curva

Speed
Velocidad

Stop
Alto

Traffic bumps
Topes

Cattle
Ganado

Gas station
Gasolinera

Gasoline
Gasolina

Regular
Nova

Super
Extra

Oil
Aceite

Air
Aire

Tire
Llanta

Fill it up, please
Lleno por favor

Straight ahead
Derecho

To the left
A la izquierda

To the right
A la derecha

Where is the highway for ___ ?
¿Dónde está el camino para ___ ?

How far is ___ ?
¿Cuántos kilómetros a ___ ?

At the Hotel *En el Hotel*

A room
Un cuarto

A single room
Un cuarto sencillo

A double room
Un cuarto doble

A triple room
Un cuarto para tres

With a view
Con vista

Without a view
Sin vista

A quiet room
Un cuarto tranquilo

With a ceiling fan
Con ventilador

Without a ceiling fan
Sin ventilador

With air conditioning
Con aire acondicionado

Bathroom
Baño

Shower
Regadera

Toilet paper
Papel sanitario

Soap
Jabón

Hot water
Agua caliente

Cold water
Agua fría

Bed
Cama

Sheet
Sábana

Pillow
Almohada

Blanket
Cobija

Towel
Toalla

How much is a ___ room?
¿Cuánto cuesta un cuarto ___ ?

Are there cheaper rooms?
¿Hay cuartos más baratos?

Does it include tax?
¿Incluye el impuesto?

─In the Long-distance Office   *En la Caseta de Larga Distancia*─

I wish to call ___ (place).
Quiero hacer una llamada a ___ .

To phone number ___ .
Al número ___ .

I wish to talk to ___ .
Quiero hablar con ___ .

With anyone answering
Con quien conteste

Collect
Por cobrar

I'll pay here.
Pago aquí.

Person calling ___ (name).
De parte de ___ .

──────── In the Restaurant   *En el Restaurant* ────────

The menu
El menu or *la carta*

A table
Una mesa

Food plate
Platillo

Ceramic plate
Plato

A fork *Un tenedor*	Breakfast *Desayuno*
A spoon *Una cuchara*	Lunch *Comida*
A knife *Un cuchillo*	Dinner *Cena*
A napkin *Una servilleta*	Lunch special *Comida corrida*
A glass of water *Un vaso de agua*	House specialty *Especialidad de la casa*
Salt *Sal*	Tip *Propina*
Pepper *Pimienta*	Tax *Impuesto*
Waitress *Mesera*	The bill *La cuenta*
Waiter *Mesero*	

——— Polite Expressions *Expresiones de Cortesía*———

Excuse me
Disculpe
(Use when you ask a question or when you excuse yourself to leave the room or the company of other people)

Excuse me
Discúlpeme or *Dispénseme*
(Use when you step on someone's toe, etc.)

Thank you
Gracias

Thank you very much
Muchas gracias or *muchísimas gracias*
(Use the latter expression for emphasis)

187

You're welcome
De nada

Repeat please
Repita por favor

I'm sorry
Lo siento

—— **Excuse Me, Where Is** ___ **?** *Dispense, ¿dónde está ___ ?*——

The ___ hotel
El hotel ___

The long-distance office
La caseta de larga distancia

The market
El mercado

The/a bank
El/un banco

___ Street
La Calle ___

A store
Una tienda

___ Avenue
La Avenida ___

A pharmacy
Una farmacia

The post office
El correo

A liquor store
Una licorería

The telegraph office
La oficina de telégrafos

A bakery
Una panadería

Postscript

If you would like to share your experiences in the Yucatán with others, please send me your comments, criticisms, and suggestions. Please address your letters to: Memo Barroso, c/o Harmony Books, One Park Avenue, New York, NY 10016.

Travel Notes

Travel Notes

Travel Notes

Travel Notes

Travel Notes

Travel Notes

Travel Notes

Travel Notes